South Bank Religion

The Diocese of Southwark 1959-1969

James Bogle

Hatcham Press

The icon reproduced on the cover, *Christ the Worker,* by John Hayward, is in the chapel at Wychcroft, the Southwark Diocesan Training Centre, Bletchingley, Surrey, and is used by kind permission.

British Library Cataloguing-in-Publication Data
A catalogue record for this book is available from the British Library

Published by
HATCHAM PRESS
8 Waller Road, London SE14 5LA

Copyright C HATCHAM PRESS 2002

ISBN 0-9543508-0-4

Printed by Creeds the Printers, Bridport, Dorset

Contents

Introduction

From 1959-1969 the Diocese of Southwark under the leadership of Bishop Mervyn Stockwood and Bishop John Robinson became a focus for reform in the Church of England and the movement received the appellation 'South Bank Religion'. Its influence through *Honest to God* became world wide. Forty years on the popular estimate of it has sunk very low.

In 1995 Valerie Pitt, who had been involved in the movement, though never uncritically, wrote:

> "What," the survivors seemed to ask, "was all that about then?" All that activity, that flamboyance, that excitement – gone like the snows of past years without so much as a mark on the pavement. Bliss it might well have been "in that dawn to be alive" and fizzing about Bristol or Cambridge or South London but – "Whatever happened to the revolution?"

Nevertheless there are 'marks on the pavement'.

A recent correspondent to *The Times* wrote of clergy of the 'liberal school of the permissive 1960's' and continued, 'Many in the Church have now moved on, having had more than enough of liberalism and the dreadful damage it has brought upon the Church. Liberalism has brought with it lower church attendances, fewer baptisms, fewer confirmations and fewer couples wanting to be married in church'.

In fact liberalism is not altogether a good description for the 1960's. Robinson positively repudiated being known as a 'liberal' and wanted to be known as a radical. The decline in congregational life began before *Honest to God* was published and it hit the conservative Diocese of London harder than the Diocese of Southwark. The cause was not 'liberalism' but secularization, especially urban secularization. This point was cogently made by Nicolas Stacey, Rector of Woolwich.

And then even some of the surviving protagonists are disenchanted at hopes unfulfilled.

It is the purpose of this book to review what was achieved in Southwark during years of 'South Bank Religion' and, briefly, to see whether it still has relevance at the present time.

I am indebted to the Rt. Revd. Ronald Bowlby, Bishop of Southwark 1981-1991, for very kindly writing a foreword; also to the Rt. Revd. David Atkinson, Canon Eric James, Canon Derek Landreth, the Very Revd. Michael Mayne, Canon W.J. Milligan, Canon G.A. Parrott, and the Revd. Dr. John Bowden who have read the text and made some valuable suggestions; and also to those who have given me interviews or corresponded. I have greatly appreciated their help and profited from it.

James Bogle

Foreword

by the Rt. Revd. Ronald Bowlby,
Bishop of Southwark 1981-1991

It has been fascinating to read this account of "South Bank Religion" and the Southwark Diocese during the 1960's. At the beginning of that period I was working on a housing estate on Tees-side, but in 1966 came to Croydon, much closer to the scene, but at that time still part of the diocese of Canterbury.

I had read *Honest to God* and, like many others, had been more encouraged than disturbed by it. I knew many of the "principal players" by name and a few of them personally. Little did I think then that I would later be asked to lead this great diocese for a few years during the aftermath of this astonishingly fertile time.

James Bogle has documented all the main developments with care and accuracy, as far as I can judge. He rightly stresses the key part played by John Robinson, not simply as the author of a major publishing sensation in 1963, but as a pastor and teacher of lasting influence in the diocese. The combination of his gifts with those of Mervyn Stockwood, who as Diocesan bishop was eager to promote new thinking and new forms of worship and church life, was one of the most potent factors in allowing so much creative experiment to take place in the diocese so quickly.

As the author rightly points out, the South Bank was not the only place where renewal was taking place, whether in liturgy and theology, or ministry and morals. The Parish and People movement, for instance, had national support and isolated initiatives had been taking place all over the country for some time. What made Southwark special was the coming together of a significant number of outstanding clergy and laity, some already in post in 1960, others drawn there by two exceptional leaders. They were determined to release the church into new life and understanding, and so into a different kind of engagement with society and a more effective kind of mission. Not all the experiments worked, as this study shows, but a surprising number did and, when I arrived in the diocese in 1981, the fruits were there to see. A generation on, it is easy to forget how imaginative and "daring" some of these seemed at the time.

Southwark remains a diocese which encourages innovation, along with a strong sense of belonging together, and not a little of that is due to the inspiring people who are remembered in these pages.

1

The Years of Stability – The 1950's

Church life in the 1950's was remarkably stable. The Archbishop of Canterbury, Geoffrey Fisher, was temperamentally disinclined to be radical. The Book of Common Prayer and the King James Version of the Bible were generally used with little question. Supplementary books of prayers for schools or private devotion were cast in collect form, in biblical idiom and in seventeenth century language even when dealing with such subjects as world peace or industry; it was not thought odd. Dean Milner-White's *Daily Prayer*, first published in 1941, but still very popular in the 1950's, was characteristic. Biblical theology, itself somewhat conservative, became dominant and was exemplified by the work of Alan Richardson. Popular theology was represented by the works of C.S. Lewis (they are still widely read) and was also conservative. The Thirty-Nine Articles were accepted as a Anglican norm and a move in Convocation to revise them found little support. Ministerial training was exclusively in small residential theological colleges mostly without links to other educational institutions. Though there was a Group for the Ordination of Women in the Church it did not command widespread support. Moral thinking was similarly conservative and the reports of the Church of England Moral Welfare Council, for instance, were generally received by Church Assembly without debate.

There were a number of stirrings in the wider Church, which, some of them, if then scarcely more than clouds no bigger than a man's hand, were to cause rough weather in time to come. In 1953 a commission was set up by Church Assembly to consider how the clergy and laity could best be joined together in the synodical government of the Church. That did not bear fruit until 1969, but was a sign of an acknowledged desire on the part of the laity to play a greater part in the government of the Church.

Stewardship reached the Church of England from America in the mid 1950's. It created much needed funding, which opened up new possibilities in the parishes, and at the same time, through Time and Talents, offered new potential of service to lay people. Stewardship was thought too sophisticated for inner city parishes; that was later shown to be a misjudgment.

An editorial in the *Church Times* in 1950, perhaps rather surprisingly, advocated the parish communion. The mood of Convocation was very cautious; the westward position, for example, could only be a rare and exceptional use and must have the permission of the bishop. Alan Ecclestone, at Darnall, in Sheffield, adopted a Parish Communion, replacing said Holy Communion and sung Mass. A number of other parishes emulated Darnall. Among them was the parish of Halton, in Leeds, where the Vicar was Ernest Southcott. Southcott introduced liturgical and pastoral reform, which he wrote of in *The Parish Comes Alive*. He held baptism services infrequently and made home visits before them, as well as having a rehearsal. He insisted on confirmed godparents. For the service the font was moved centrally. Members of the ordinary congregation came and a sermon was preached. Later there was a follow up. On Sunday mornings there was a conflation of mattins and parish communion and in the evening a mission service. For the eucharist there was a full offertory procession with cross and candles. The Prayer for the Church Militant was read by a layman. The Collect for Purity and the Prayer of Humble Access were said congregationally, as was the Prayer of Oblation after the Prayer of Consecration. Westward position was adopted. A parish breakfast followed the parish communion. But it was not so much for the parish communion that Halton was distinguished as for its house churches. Mass was said daily in different houses. It became a part of pastoral strategy that services were held even in the homes of the unconfirmed. A special effort was made once a year, so that in the month of October 1952 100 homes in the parish had house celebrations. Home meetings in the evenings attracted as many as 1000 different people. The strategy clearly depended on the assumption that parishioners retained Christian loyalty, that they were 'lapsed'. Nevertheless the ministry was remarkable.

Even so, at the end of the decade, parish communions were not widespread. As Dean of Clare College, Cambridge, John Robinson made liturgical innovations which he recorded in *Liturgy Coming to Life*. Robinson was critical of the usual 8 o'clock service of Holy Communion, which he regarded as individualistic, pietistic, subjective and unrelated to the world where redemption was meant to be taking place. He wanted to throw emphasis, not on what was said, but what was done in the eucharist and, following Dom Gregory Dix, stressed the fourfold action of taking, blessing, breaking and sharing. The eucharist was a corporate act, in which every worshipper had his or her own liturgy. The priest or priests facing the people witnessed to this corporateness. He used modern translations of the Bible for the greater contemporary impact. Robinson was insistent that the bread and wine used in the eucharist should be everyday bread and wine, related to the everyday world and expressing concern for it, even for economic and political matters, though it hardly seems that this usage would bear the weight he hoped it would. And the service at Clare was ecumenical, in a way unusual at that time, though admittedly reflecting the special circumstances of a college chapel. Interestingly in the light of his later position, he made a strong plea for adult baptism, confirmation and the eucharist to be thrown together as a single initiatory rite; this he practised when he went to Southwark.

Robinson had also written prophetically about theological training. Shortly after he relinquished his post as Chaplain to Wells Theological College in 1952, he had contributed an article to *Theology* on the need for change in theological training.

The coming pattern of [the Church of England's] ministry is bound to be largely non-professional, in the sense that its priesthood will consist in great proportion of men working at secular jobs at every level, both manual and administrative... For the training of such a non-professional ministry the existing theological college set-up would be virtually irrelevant. For it is essential that it must be done *without* taking men out of the jobs and milieu in which they are. The experience of the trades unions in training their leadership through night classes, summer schools, Ruskin College, etc., should give the church something to work on.'[1]

A movement in ministry was pioneered by Donald Coggan, then Bishop of Bradford, and Southcott; they drew attention to the need for priests to be trained in pastoral counselling and commended the work of Dr. Frank Lake. Lake was a returned medical missionary who had trained in psychiatry. He tended to emphasize the importance of the earliest months and years of life in the formation of personality, owing debts to Harry Guntrip and Melanie Klein, but all the major schools of psychiatry were studied. Where Jung had spoken of self-realisation, Lake wished to offer a distinctively Christian psychiatry, to seek Christ-realisation for the person counselled, placing Christ in the centre of the field of vision and pointing to his offer of a New Being through new relationships with God in him. By the early 1960's groups of clergy and psychiatrists were formed nationwide. There was considerable mutual distrust between clergy and psychiatrists to be overcome. In 1962 the Clinical Theology Association was formed at Nottingham with a staff of psychiatrists and clergy and Lake as Director.

In 1946 there had been formed a movement to bring Christian understanding and action to public affairs, political, economic and social. This was Christian Action, led by John Collins, at that time Dean of Oriel College, Oxford, and later Canon of St. Paul's Cathedral. It commanded wide support. Christian Action took up a number of issues; one of its most effective actions was against hanging, joining with the Campaign for the Abolition of Capital Punishment in 1955. It was years before the bishops came round and years again before the Government did. But the movement prevailed in the end.

Already in 1950 the Vicar of St. George in the East, Stepney, Jack Boggis, had felt he must protest on behalf of African seamen who, of necessity, were living in grossly overcrowded conditions. The Bishop of London, William Wand, had noticed them in congregations and urged that they be made welcome. Race relations continued to be a matter of concern throughout the 1950's and this concern came to a head after race riots at Notting Hill and Nottingham in 1958. Both Convocations debated the presence and growth of multi-racial communities early in 1959. Both synods noted the difficulties of employment and housing which 'coloured immigrants' were facing, though there was little constructive suggestion about what might be done. Both urged that 'coloured people' be welcomed as members of the churches and be given hospitality in church members' homes. The limitation of immigrants was raised in the Convocation of York, but rejected on the ground that it would be construed as discrimination. Church people seem to have wanted to show good will, but there was little positive action.

1. *Theology* June 1952 pp 203f

2

Church Life Renewed

These stirrings of renewal, clouds which might build up to herald a storm, did in fact burst in the 1960's. In some matters change was expected, even overdue; in others it came as a surprise. The decade was one of much innovation throughout the Church. The acknowledged centre of it was the Diocese of Southwark and the movement of reform soon came to be known as 'South Bank Religion'. Although the scope of innovation was large, including the articulation of the faith, liturgical change, renewed patterns of church life and ministry, moral thinking, even church design and church music – all were found, often initiated, in Southwark.

Mervyn Stockwood accepted the bishopric of Southwark in November 1958. He had spent nineteen years in the parish of St. Matthew, Moorfields, Bristol, followed by four remarkably successful years at the University Church, Great St. Mary's, Cambridge. Very shortly after his appointment as Bishop of Southwark was made public he preached a sermon at Great St. Mary's with his thoughts for the future. It is evident that for him success was important. He asked: 'How can the church come alongside the people? If a bishop found himself talking to a working man standing on a wharf on the Thames what language could he use to get over to the man the idea that he was an apostle, commissioned by God to further a movement, and the society that existed for the purpose was the Church, and the sooner he, the working man, got into the Church the better?' He looked for a more flexible type of church organization. 'When people can see, for example, that the Communion Service is tied up with what happens in the factory, in the home, in the Trade Union meeting and on the City Council, the Prayer Book and what it stands for begin to come to life.' In particular he looked for worker priests – 'men who will stay on the ground floor, earning their livings as factory hands, bus drivers, railwaymen, Trade Union officials, shopkeepers and schoolmasters'. Then he asked himself: 'What has my Cambridge ministry taught me? Many things, but one in particular – the necessity to express Christian doctrine in meaningful language, which involves taking into account contemporary thinking' [1]. The concern for the secular world and the twice repeated concern for relevant language is noteworthy.

As Stockwood was coming to Southwark the bishopric of Woolwich was falling vacant. Within weeks of his own acceptance of the work of diocesan he approached John Robinson to accept the position as his suffragan. Robinson had been his curate at St. Matthew's, then on the staff of Wells Theological College and more recently Dean of Clare College, Cambridge. They had always kept in touch and were close friends. In writing to the Archbishop of Canterbury, Geoffrey Fisher, about the matter Stockwood said:

> I want as Bishop of Woolwich a man who (1) understands what I am trying to do (2) who has the intellectual competence and theological knowledge to advise me (3) who is accustomed to dealing with and teaching ordinands (4) who while his special concern will be for experimental work can at the same time do the normal pastoral and routine duties of a suffragan bishop. At Southwark there is a strongish team at the centre – three archdeacons, the Bishop of Kingston and the Provost. I have already established happy relationships with most of them and I know they will be a great help to me. But all of them are essentially conventional Churchmen. I use the word "conventional" in no unkindly sense, but to describe an attitude. Within the existing frame of reference they will be friends and guides to me and I shall be able to talk things over with them. But in addition to these six men I want a seventh, the new Bishop

of Woolwich, who while realising the importance of the conventional approach in large areas of the diocese, will appreciate the need for a new approach in places like Rotherhithe and Bermondsey... The new Bishop of Woolwich should be a man who, although a competent pastor and capable of doing routine duties, will be qualified to help me tackle this tremendous problem – how to win to Christ the thousands and thousands of people in districts like Bermondsey and Rotherhithe to whom Christianity means nothing. [2]

Stockwood wrote of what he was trying to do. What was it? Michael De-la-Noy comments, 'almost certainly a reference to his desire to set up as soon as possible a new form of training for the ministry'.[3] This is surely right – see qualification (3) in his job specification for the new Bishop of Woolwich and the fact that in due course Robinson had episcopal responsibility for the Southwark Ordination Course; nevertheless it is much too narrow. Stockwood's missionary purpose (which came to be fully shared by his new suffragan) can be expressed much more broadly as a desire for *aggiornamento* (as it came to be called after the Second Vatican Council) especially directed at the industrialised parts of the diocese. It was true in the pattern of ministry; it was true in liturgy; it was true in the expression of the faith; it was true in pastoral matters; and it was true in the pattern of church life.

In his enthronement sermon in May 1959 Stockwood spoke of the need for vision – his text was, 'where there is no vision the people perish'. He spoke of the need for the church to be concerned with every aspect of the nation's life, ridding itself of the dichotomy of sacred and secular. He upheld the parochial system, from his own experience, but looked for a supplement to it. 'I should like to see cautious experiments with a new type of priesthood and a new type of organization. Is it possible that a man who works in industry and is also ordained will be better

16

able to understand the needs and outlook of his associates than one who, because of his status as a parochial clergyman, is inevitably, to some extent, segregated? And is it possible that for some industrial workers the expression of Christian community may become more meaningful if it is set free from the parochial system?' Turning to the relationship between dogma and truth, he asked, 'How can we express [the faith] in words that are meaningful to a contemporary generation and take into consideration other branches of knowledge and categories of thought? We should not be afraid to admit that, while we accept without compromise the basic concepts of the Christian revelation, there are many things about which we are ignorant and must reserve our judgement, many things in human experience that seem to contradict our claims, and come what may we will follow where truth leads and always be intellectually honest and spiritually humble.' [4]

An important part of Stockwood's strategy for the diocese was to set up informal clergy teams or groups in certain riverside areas. He had alluded to this in his letter for the Southwark Diocesan Leaflet in November of the same year. He looked for teams of as many as ten priests in a large parish, of which three would be full time pastors in the accepted sense while seven would earn their livings in the secular world, though not necessarily priest-workmen as the term was commonly understood. He hoped that the members of a team would be willing to remain in the same place for at least ten years. The ten clergymen would try to be active in the whole life of the district – industrial, social, recreational, civic, educational. They might make use of informal house churches. Clergy groups and teams were set up in riverside parishes; in Bermondsey, led by F.S. (Bill) Skelton; in Woolwich, led by Nicolas Stacey; and, later, in Deptford, led by David Diamond. There was also a group led by W.J.(Barney) Milligan at Eltham. Woolwich became the best known. Stacey was a priest of great ability, a dynamic leader, an

Olympic athlete, a mixture of the gracious and the assertive, with a talent for journalism and a deep concern for the reform of the organisation of the church. After a curacy at Portsea he served as Chaplain to the Bishop of Birmingham and was appointed Rector of Woolwich at the early age of 31. He soon assembled a team of able, dedicated and hard working clergy for the parish. It was not long before the great church of St Mary Magdalen was transfomed with a creche for babies, a lunch-time snack bar, an all day coffee bar and the galleries turned into a variety of rooms for meetings and exhibitions. Later a discotheque opened in the crypt with a licensed bar. Rooms in the church were also offered to the Greenwich Council of Social Service (a voluntary body) and the Citizens Advice Bureau. The Quadrant Housing Association had its offices there. A homeless family was invited to move into the clergy house. It was not all well received. An incumbent in another part of the diocese wrote in his parish magazine, 'If Stacey thinks he can build the Kingdom of God by frying eggs on the altar and percolating coffee in the organ pipes he should think again.' The intended effect, however, that large numbers of people should use the building each week, was achieved. The conversion of the building inspired others, including that of St. Catherine's, Hatcham, which attracted considerable attention.

The advent of Stanley Evans meant another radical voice in the diocese. Throughout his ministry he had served in deprived parishes in east London, the last (his only incumbency) being Holy Trinity, Dalston. Although he had abandoned his communism after the invasion of Hungary in 1956, he still remained very much a Christian socialist and a sympathizer with the countries of the Eastern Bloc. He was appointed Chancellor of the Cathedral, Principal of the Southwark Ordination Course (of which more below) and Director of Post-Ordination Training. This latter, though it had existed in a minimal form before, took a big step forward under Evans' direction and a further step forward under that of Derek Tasker, to become one of the most thorough courses in the country. In-service training for incumbents was also developed. In October 1961 Evans gave a series of lectures to clergy and church workers in the Chapter House of the Cathedral under the title *The Church in the Back Streets*, a subject very familiar to him and, it may be thought, dear to his heart. He began by saying,'All the inner ring of South London, in the back streets of large cities and towns all over the country, there are parish churches staffed by devoted clergy which, in any ordinary sense of the word, have failed.' That was remarkably like what Nicolas Stacey at Woolwich was to say three years later, but it does not seem to have caused any comment. Evans illustrated what he had to say with the example of a local chuch which had struggled for a full century to minister to the poor in its area and which had finally given up the struggle and closed. Evans saw no easy solutions, but he regarded certain things as essential in such a ministry, humility, readiness to learn and service. For the outreach of such a church he commended advice centres; youth work; old people's clubs; and caring for the mentally ill. These were worthwhile suggestions at a time when many churches undertook no social action at all. He looked for a participatory liturgy and a participatory church. The back-street parson needed to be strongly involved in the community.

A Director of Religious Sociology for the diocese was appointed by Stockwood in 1965, Leslie Harman; he had been involved in social work both before and after his ordination. This was the first such appointment in the Church of England. The intention was that there should be a parish-by-parish survey with the object of enabling the church to plan its own structure and strategy more realistically and to discover how it could better serve the needs of the community. Most dioceses now have a full time social responsibility officer. Stockwood also appointed a Press Officer, Norman Hood. Part of his job was to edit the diocesan journal, *The Bridge*; he was also very effective in taking up journalistic issues nationally. Most dioceses now also have designated press officers, either full-time or part-time.

After four years in office, in July 1963, Stockwood returned to his purpose for the diocese in an article in the *Evening Standard* entitled *South Bank Religion – What I'm Trying to Do*. Shortly before, the Diocesan Evangelical Clergy Association had let it be known that some members were very upset about four things. There was the publication of *Honest to God*; sermons given by Douglas Rhymes at the Cathedral pleading for a new moral code; a protest by John Pearce-Higgins concerning the Thirty-Nine Articles; and a requiem service for Pope John XXIII at which Stockwood had been both celebrant and preacher. In his article Stockwood described how he had recently flown over London by night; he reminded his readers of the responsibility which he and the Bishop of London shared for one tenth of the population of England, where church attendances were lower than anywhere in the country. On his appointment as Bishop of Southwark he had decided that new methods would have to be used to break down the barrier of misunderstanding and apathy. Stockwood noted that John Pearce-Higgins' protest against assent to the Thirty-Nine Articles of Religion was not new. Distinguished churchmen had done so before. In *Honest to God* the Bishop of Woolwich was looking for a bridge between the sacred and the secular. Stockwood refused to join in a witch-hunt and cited the tolerant views of a distinguished predecessor, Cyril Garbett, later Archbishop of York. Over Rhymes' sermons on sexual morality, stressing less outer acts, more inner relationships, Stockwood wrote that he had some reservations, but welcomed sensible discussion. He held that it was his job as bishop to foster wise experiment while shepherding those who found it difficult to accept new ways. 'Superficial criticisms, hysterical denunciations and smug pharisaism will not hinder me from lending support to my priests who, no matter what their limitations may be, are trying to make Christ and His Church a reality to the people of South London.'[5]

Although the standards of pastoral care at Woolwich were high, the actual number of worshippers did not greatly increase. There had been about 50 in the congregation when Stacey first came to Woolwich; after 4 1/2 years there were still only about 100, the increase mostly from the socially more superior areas outside the parish. He had set himself a target of 400. This was a matter of great concern to him. He was offered the opportunity to write an article in the colour supplement of the *Observer* in December 1964, which was entitled *A Mission's Failure*. 'For 4 1/2 years in Thames-side Woolwich I have been head of one of the largest and ablest teams of clergy in any parish in England. We have had a remarkable opportunity of making a breakthrough in getting people to come to church. We have played every card in the pack. We have done everything we set out to do. But we have achieved virtually not one of the modest things we hoped for... We have quite obviously failed.'[6] He did not say what the modest things the team hoped to achieve were, apart from increasing the congregation. Other than its title and its opening paragraphs the article was innocuous enough, with an account of much useful caring activity. It provoked a huge response, perhaps partly because by then anything at all controversial from Southwark elicited a strong reaction, perhaps also because the secularism of the sixties was beginning to bite and it touched a raw nerve. Some, of a radical turn of mind, were supportive and there were fellow clergy relieved that St. Mary's Woolwich, with all its advantages of staffing and publicity, did little better than the norm. Most who responded, from archbishops to lay people, were opposed, even hostile. Stockwood wrote in the Diocesan Leaflet of 'the apparent failures' of the work at Woolwich. He rejected simple explanations and was driven to ask 'Why do men appear to respond more readily in Reigate, Purley and Coulsdon than in Walworth, Woolwich and Battersea?' He could not supply an answer. He did not pass adverse comment on

Stacey's article, but he did not like talk of failure. The Archbishop of Canterbury, Michael Ramsey, wrote, 'As soon as this sort of success or failure discussion starts, by its very nature it secularises the issue.' Stacey himself summed up, 'This may be an exaggeration but I sense that since my article nobody any longer expects a working class parish to come alive in the traditional way.' In a television interview he said he thought that orthodox methods would no longer work. He foresaw a great stripping down of the Church in which there would be far fewer church buildings, in which the Church would cease to be a great state of the realm, and in which most clergy would be earning their livings in secular activities. There would be little cells of Christians meeting in each other's homes and only rarely going to places of worship. A little later Stacey developed his ideas in a further article in *The Observer*. He reiterated his belief that most clergy in full time parochial employment should be encouraged to take secular work and also that there should be a massive reduction in churches and chapels. He considered that a church which was really committed to serving humanity should give away its money – for the Church of England, the holdings of the Church Commissioners. 'One of the most pressing social problems in Britain today is the integration of the immigrant population. This can be achieved only by massive dispersal from the ghettos. A Church charitable fund would be able to buy houses all over Britain for this purpose.'[7] Though the aim is very questionable the idea of the Church Commissioners using assets for charity was precursory to the Church Urban Fund. He concluded, 'This cellular movement will require the maximum of trained articulate laity and a minimum of paid clergy, organizations and buildings. Indeed there is no reason why Christians should not hire the local school for an hour on Sunday for their act of worship.'

There were in fact clear successes at Woolwich. The clergy team, though legally Rector and Curates, was certainly different from the conventional relationship, not only in that its members worked on team decisions rather than those of an individual, but also in the length of stay in the parish. It was thus much nearer to the pattern of the later Team Ministries set up under the Pastoral Measure, to which it formed a precursor.

Ecumenical endeavour was remarkable. Very shortly after he arrived Stacey played a big part in the formation of a new Woolwich and District Council of Churches. A Methodist minister, Ray Billington, who had worked closely with the Anglican team, was invited, at the end of his three years at the local Methodist church, to join the clergy at St. Mary's working as an industrial chaplain and teaching. The Parochial Church Council petitioned the diocesan bishop to agree to Billington preaching, taking services at St. Mary's, other than Holy Communion, administering the chalice at Holy Communion, and he and his wife receiving communion themselves. All this Stockwood agreed to except administering the chalice, which he told the council he did not have authority to do, though that also was agreed to later. This step was not without opposition from the conservative. Even more ambitious was a scheme for sharing the church with the Woolwich Presbyterian congregation. Their church was huge, their congregation small. In 1962 John Robinson preached the sermon at the Tercentenary Service of the Presbyterian Church in Woolwich and suggested that a good way of celebrating would be to return to the ancient parish church from which they had been ejected three hundred years before. St. Mary's would be more than adequate for both Anglicans and Presbyterians. Sunday morning services would be separate, while the hope would be that evening services could be held together. The first intentions quickly foundered on ecclesiastical law, unchanged since the days of the Presbyterian ejection in 1662. This was the more frustrating since those keenest on ecumenism in the British Council of Churches were holding up Woolwich as a pattern to be followed throughout the country. Stacey wrote to the Archbishop, who promised to raise the matter in Convocation. A Commission was set up and after eighteen months it produced its report, *Sharing of Churches*. It was grudging towards the Free Churches. If one of them were to share an Anglican church their congregation would have no security of tenure. No joint ownership of churches, even in new areas, was permitted. A Parish and People group involving Stacey and Robinson produced a much more radical unofficial report which was circulated to the members of Convocation (Robinson had been elected a Proctor in 1960) prior to the debate on *Sharing of Churches*. The debate led to the setting up of a new commission on which Robinson sat, bringing to it his intimate knowledge of the situation at Woolwich. When that commission's report was debated in Convocation in 1967, it was still found inadequate and Eric James, a Southwark Proctor in Convocation, moved an amendment to make clearly possible 'the sharing of buildings by Churches as equal partners', in effect allowing new jointly owned churches to be built. The Bill which in due course went through Parliament incorporated most of the recommendations of the Parish and People report, which had been warmly welcomed and approved in Convocation. In retrospect this was a major ecumenical advance and it is no coincidence that it was just the kind of issue for which Stacey had a passionate concern. As well as a Methodist minister and a Presbyterian congregation, with their minister, a Baptist minister was invited to join the team, as a housing manager. To complete the ecclesiastical spectrum, in 1967 a Roman Catholic priest came, Fr.Henri du Halgouet. The difficulties were very great, and he received only 'qualified permission' from the Archbishop of Southwark, so that he had a teaching job in a local girls' comprehensive school and did no more than join the others in prayer, fellowship and social work. Such an ecumenical tem was unique and its formation in itself a remarkable achievement. Latterly the parish also was very unusual, and a model for the future, in that some of the clergy earned their living in secular employment, mostly in educational work, while for a short time a paid bursar was employed for parochial administration.

There were other successes. Stacey had a marked (though not exclusive) leaning towards the practical outworking of religion. Thus at a civic service not long after he came to the parish he could say that in the last forty years the Labour Party in Woolwich had done more to build the Kingdom of God than the official Church had done. (The Labour Party was mentioned not because of his personal political conviction, but because they had been the party in power on the Council) Indeed the Council had been the agent of much good and the Church weak. Stacey set about to do what he could to rectify the situation. A branch of the Samaritans was begun; it is still serving those in distress. A major concern was homelessness. Constant appeals for help would come to him as Rector. Together with friends he began a housing association, Quadrant. It became distinctive by converting smaller, two storey properties in poorer areas. Most associations converted larger three or four storey properties, but the older two storey houses with extended backs made two good flats at a reasonable cost. Secondly Stacey managed to negotiate Local Authority (Greater London Council) loans for conversions; this enabled conversions to proceed at a much faster rate, so that by the end of the sixties some 400 dwellings a year were made available. Quadrant became one of the largest and most successful housing associations. Another concern was the setting up of a Family Planning Association clinic in a huge reception centre for the homeless in Plumstead. It soon became much used.

So Stacey could say, 'I am still desparately anxious to see all the reforms for which Parish and People and others stand, not because I think they will solve our problems, but because they will expose the real ones more clearly... The inescapable fact, as I see it, is of the ever-increasing alienation of modern man from the Church.' His *Observer* article was not unconsidered. He had written in much the same vein in a long memorandum to the

Bishop of Woolwich two years before. He stressed how dependent community involvement was on the clergy, and that the attempt to care pastorally for every one in the parish was a crippling strain on their energy. He was not over flattering about the existing congregation. Quite soon after the Woolwich team had been set up Valerie Pitt, a sharp observer, noted its ethos was 'de haut en bas'. A parishioner wrote that, 'it was not surprising that, despite Mr. Stacey's assurances that their help was needed, many hung back, feeling perhaps that better qualified people were now at hand to do the jobs they had previously done.' Stacey himself wrote 'We found very little indigenous lay leadership... inevitably it was for the clergy to lead' and a former member of staff has commented, 'it was not of the people, it was at the people and to the people.' A strong highly intelligent team of clergy needs to make a very great effort to allow lay people to take responsibiity within the life of a church and to carry a congregation with it. It may not have been a coincidence that the Bingo and the Samaritans, which both had substantial lay involvement, both flourished.

A Mission's Failure did represent the beginning of a loss of confidence. One member of the team, the Methodist, Ray Billington, had plainly become disillusioned with ordinary church life when he wrote in *Prism* in July 1965. Those of a like mind in the Keble Group and Parish and People were less sure that the reforms they pressed for would result in success. By 1965 Eric James found himself having to justify 'South Bank Religion' in the face of distrust or hostility. In 1968, after nine years at Woolwich, Stacey resigned as Rector to become Deputy Director of Oxfam. He continued both his church ministry and secular jobs to which he brought his innovatory gifts. It was a pattern which he had advocated while still in full time paid ministry. As he left the parish he commented that the activites that emanated from St.Mary's Woolwich had been admired by visitors from all over the world; 2,500 people were using the building each week. 'What I do care about desparately is having the opportunity of trying to build God's Kingdom of love in a sad, sick and suffering world.' There can be little doubt that he and the team had seized the opportunity to fulfil that purpose in Woolwich.

Stockwood, though, was not lightly to be deterred. He wrote in a letter to the Bishop of London, Robert Stopford:

After the meeting at Lambeth a member of the Commission said to me, "I sympathize with you, Bishop, but the problems you raised in your remarks are insoluble. There is no answer to them." Robert, if this is true you and I had better pack our bags. Are we to admit that the Church in the Inner Ring is bound to fail? I refuse to accept this dismal conclusion. I believe that if we had the freedom to use our men, our resources and our plant as dictated by common sense, we could create oases of life in an existing desert.[8]

The development at Bermondsey was led by Skelton, who had been Chaplain at Clare College, Cambridge, and became Rector of St. Mary Magdalen. The ministry was a group rather than a team. The staff of five parish churches were involved, together with Michael Whinney from the Cambridge University Mission, and Methodist ministers, Jo Jones, of the Methodist Central Hall, and Clifford Johnson, of the Bermondsey Settlement; within the group some showed more commitment than others. There were valuable contacts with the local Roman Catholics . The pattern of ministry was looser than Woolwich. Stacey's Portsea experience, which had moulded him pastorally and which to a degree he reproduced (even if the pattern of decision making at Woolwich was completely different), was lacking. Nevertheless there was considerable common life in Bermondsey. Ecumenical services for the group as a whole were held regularly. An ecumenical open air procession of witness and service attracted widespread support on Good Friday. Marriage preparation was undertaken jointly; it lasted several weeks and included contributions by a doctor and an accountant.

Stockwood encouraged meetings from time to time between the Bermondsey group and the Woolwich team and ideas were shared. In Bermondsey house churches were formed, though they tended to be transitory. Woolwich also had house churches, but they too did not fulfil the hopes with which they were set up, in spite of careful preparation. In Bermondsey parish training weekends, from Friday evening till Sunday afternoon were found valuable, as were weekday evening meetings, similar to those at Woolwich, and those held by Alan Ecclestone at Darnall. Revised services of baptism were used and considerable care taken over preparation for baptism, in which lay people from the congregations were involved. Services of Parish Communion were introduced and a revised liturgy, based on that devised by Robinson for Clare College, Cambridge, was used at St. Mary's. Lay people would join in Bible study and in criticism of the sermon, and there was a sense of being involved in ministry. Christian Stewardship, imported from America, had been found valuable in suburban congregations; it was also tried successfully in Bermondsey and Woolwich, which paved the way for its use in other inner city parishes. Pastoral work in industry, under the auspices of the South London Industrial Mission, was also important in both locations; Christopher Byers, curate at St. Mary's, gave much time to it at the Courage brewery, the Alaska fur factory and elsewhere and so did John Chater, Vicar of St. Anne's, Bermondsey, at Pearce Duffs. Youth work flourished; it was a time when teenagers were readily clubbable and hundreds would meet each week. In nearby Camberwell Eric James was involved in the setting up of a study of juvenile delinquency by the Cambridge Institute of Criminology, which study continued for many years. A number of the staff at Bermondsey, including Skelton, took up secular employment after leaving the parish, as also happened at Woolwich. Although the Bermondsey ministry did not receive the attention which Woolwich did, the work was well founded and there too the congregations received a clear new lease of life and hope. The group served as a positive precursor for future formal Group Ministries.

Bermondsey also saw the development of a visionary project to provide for the lonely. Considerable property in Bermondsey and Rotherhithe was owned by the Carr-Gomm family of which Richard Carr-Gomm was a member. He served as an officer with the Coldstream Guards during the 1939-45 war and for ten years thereafter. He gradually developed a very strong Christian faith and also a great concern for those living in poverty and isolation in South London. He offered to work as a home help in Bermondsey to learn more. In November 1955 he decided to buy a house for the lonely. Loneliness would be the sole qualification; old, young, handicapped – all would be welcome. After much persuasion the house was filled. He counted on neighbourliness, so that neighbours helped with the cleaning; there were tea parties and sing songs. On the front door was the simple word 'Push' to encourage people to drop in. The vision was soon shared. Two years later there were five houses and the Abbeyfield Society was officially formed.

Expansion was extrememly rapid, so that by 1963 180 houses had been begun. There was even one at Morpeth Terrace in Westminster, which, by virtue of the finances involved, demanded its own separate society, the Morpeth Society. Tensions began to develop within the Abbeyfield Society between those who wished simply to provide accommodation as boarding or guest houses for the elderly and those who, like Carr-Gomm himself, kept to the ideal of overcoming loneliness with neighbourliness for people of all ages. There was a split; after an interval there was a re-start, of the Carr-Gomm Society, providing housing for lonely people of all ages, while the Abbeyfield concentrated on the elderly. It is a measure of the modesty of Carr-Gomm that he questioned the use of his name for this new society. Their first house, again in Bermondsey, was opened in 1965. Again expansion followed, though not so rapidly. Happily in due course there was a reconciliation between Carr-Gomm and the Abbeyfield Society. After it he wrote, 'The aim, to help the lonely – is there in all the societies (Abbeyfield, Carr-Gomm and Morpeth). The method of small units with a degree of unobtrusive care and the principles of looking on everyone as whole people – each with a body, mind and spirit – helping them to grow into their fullness by living their own lives within a friendly neighbourhood – are all the same. The societies are not in competition, there is room in the world for them each to be themselves.' The scope of the societies is now international.

The Eltham Group, led by Milligan, Vicar of All Saints, New Eltham, was wholly Anglican, eight churches with more or less a common churchmanship, and it formed a sub-deanery to the borough deanery of Greenwich. Members of the team met regularly and were mutually supportive. All the churches had a parish communion and baptisms were administered at it in the front of the church in view of the congregation. Candidates for confirmation from all the parishes were prepared together. So were couples before their marriages. One priest, Derek Watson, while curate of All Saints, worked with SLIM in the local firm of W.F. Stanley. One remarkable enterprise was undertaken by the Group after the Anglican Congress at Toronto in 1963, of which the theme was Mutual Responsibility and Interdependence. The Bishop of the Windward Islands was invited to send a curate to the subdeanery to work there and at the same time study for a London University B.D. The Group raised enough money to cover fares, fees, board and lodging. The priest who came, Sehon Goodridge, later returned to Southwark Diocese as Principal of the Simon of Cyrene Theological Institute before returning to the Windward Islands as himself Bishop.

There was notable ecumenical activity at Roehampton, where Gerald Hudson was Vicar. The 60's saw a very large London County Council housing development in the parish and new

Anglican and Methodist churches were proposed to serve the estate. This seemed a wasteful duplication, and instead very close co-operation was developed with the Methodists and the church was shared, even though it remained (necessarily) in the ownership of the Methodists. There was a joint pastoral team and complete integration of children's and youth work.

Byers, one of the curates at Bermondsey, made a plea in *Prism* to respond to secularisation in a parochial situation by using the minimum of church plant. The norm should be house churches. Anticipating Stacey he wrote, 'on festival occasions such as Christmas, Easter and Whitsun the community centre, a school or a church school would be booked for special gatherings of all Christians in the community. This should not prove difficult to arrange years in advance. Baptisms would be held once or twice a year. Confirmation, like Ordination, would take place in the Cathedral of the diocese.' He did not wish to suggest shutting down churches with reasonable congregations and workable plant, 'but that is not to say that we should continue to turn a blind eye to the work of organisations like the "Friends of Friendless Churches". Somehow that kind of misplaced enthusiasm must be directed to where it can do less damage, for example, among derelict railway stations in the post-Beeching era.'[9] Byers considered that there must be many areas in new estates and among the back streets where such a scheme as he had outlined could be tried with profit.

Stockwood also protested at the over-provision of churches and took Deptford as an example. In that sub-deanery there were 8 parish churches, three daughter churches and a mission hall served by 22 clergy and other workers. The Roman Catholics had just one church, and it was estimated that their Sunday congregations were double the combined attendance at Anglican places of worship. 'Instead of using our resources sensibly to spread the gospel and run the church efficiently, we are squandering our energies and money upon preserving the fabric,'

Stockwood wrote. 'There must be fewer and larger units well staffed and adequately financed.' When it came to new areas similar principles applied. 'Think for a moment, of the absurdity of the housing estate at Abbey Wood in the borough of Greenwich. In order to get the stipend of a clergyman to work in the area I have had to build the William Temple Church. Nothing could be more irrelevant; nothing could be further removed from the spirit and teaching of William Temple. What I need on the estate is a building like the one in Wimbledon [that of the Guild of Social Welfare] with flats for specialist clergy and laity. By all means have a small place of worship in the building, but what is more important is the wherewithall with which to engage a team of competent men.'[10]

Elections to the Convocations fell due in November 1964. Those anxious for reform made strenuous efforts to get returned. There was then a considerable number of junior clergy, curates, who met from time to time for training. The suggestion was made that one curate should be chosen to stand for election and that the other curates should support him. Four names were proposed and Adrian Esdaile, from the parish of Wimbledon, was chosen. Robinson considered that he stood no chance whatsoever and that his nomination could turn out to be a slap in the face for him and all the curates. In the event Esdaile was the clear leader overall in the election, causing considerable embarassment. The younger clergy of the diocese had shown their strength and Esdaile was to speak on a number of reforming issues in the forthcoming sessions. Also elected to Church Assembly was the very articulate and perceptive Valerie Pitt, a teacher of English Literature at Woolwich Polytechnic, who had already made her mark in *Prism* and in the *Church Times*.

In 1948 Colin Cuttell had been appointed 'Diocesan Industrial Missioner'; this was the formal beginning of what was to become the South London Industrial Mission. Cuttell was still Industrial Missioner when Stockwood came to the diocese. Robert Gibson was appointed Cuttell's successor from 1962-7; and he in turn was succeeded by Peter Challen. Throughout the sixties the Mission's work centred on factory visiting, on group work and on conferences, run from the Industrial Mission Centre at Christ Church, Blackfriars, opened in 1960. The visiting was carried out partly by full time chaplains and partly by chaplains who had other pastoral responsibilities. Although it was Anglican led, it was ecumenical. The dominant, though not the only, figure in SLIM's group work was Cecilia Goodenough, the Diocesan Lay Missioner. The groups' themes varied – industrial, social, political, topical, religious and directly biblical matters were included – and Cecilia Goodenough liked to ground them in scripture. She had a great concern for housing and homelessness. In the early 1960's the subjects were general – Decisions, Politics, Authority. As the decade progressed the themes became more specific and directly related to current industrial affairs, e.g. Prices and Incomes Policy legislation, or to contemporary theology, e.g. Harvey Cox's *Secular City*. Cecilia Goodenough devised an exhibition based on the Lordship of Christ as Prophet, Priest, Shepherd and King which was displayed in churches and factories and aroused interest and a lively response. Conferences were held at Worthing. At the beginning of the decade there were four in the year, with 35 at each one, but support had noticeably diminished by 1968 to no more than 50 in total. The theme of all four 1959-60 conferences was 'Christian Responsibility in Industry', but the themes of later conferences changed to reflect industrial conflict and a greater stress on social justice. In October 1968 SLIM, in conjunction with the Cathedral, organised a 'Festival of Industry' incorporating an Industrial Thanksgiving Service and four Sunday night sessions at the Cathedral under the titles 'Work, Leisure and Community', 'Fear of Change', 'Participation and Decision Making' and 'Authority and Human Dignity'. The stance of SLIM never polarised politically and there was a continuing endeavour to address both management and workers. SLIM saw its work as support for wealth creation; that term was later to become much more popular (and politicised).

When Stockwood came to Southwark he did not have experience of industry, although his sympathies with ordinary working people from his parochial work in Bristol were well known. In his enthronement address he called on the Church to rid itself "of the dichotomy of sacred and secular." He wanted to see working men ordained. There was a difference here with Cuttell, who had set himself against worker priests. Stockwood did take an interest in SLIM – he spent a day with apprentices at Greyladies, the Diocesan House on Blackheath, for instance, and took part in one of SLIM's weekend conferences on industrial relations; he also met with national and local Trade Union officials. He asked Robert Gibson as Senior Chaplain of SLIM for his opinion on what was to become a seminal book – E.F. Schumacher's *Small is Beautiful*. Nevertheless industrial mission was for him no more than a handmaid to the parochial system. Robinson by contrast saw SLIM as a clear outworking of 'Being the Church in the World'. Even before his consecration he spoke to the Industrial Advisory Council, the controlling body of SLIM, about the Bishop of Southwark's plans, which he was to administer. 'The Bishop said his first intention was to try and put men into industry as part of their training for the priesthood, and the Council was reassured about that part of the plan.' Robinson acted as Chairman of the Industrial Advisory Council from 1966 until he returned to Cambridge. Another leader of note was Ernest Southcott, the Provost of the Cathedral, who became Chairman of the Executive of SLIM in 1962.

SLIM's visiting represented a major undertaking in pastoral work, even if, by its very nature, it is difficult to assess. In 1960 the idea of chaplains visiting in industrial concerns was widely acceptable. In some instances it led on to a new set of concerns for the parish church, as at St. Peter's Battersea where the Vicar, Peter Duncan, visited industries, created house churches and used the church buildings as a community centre. Compare also Woolwich Parish Church where a curate, Robert Hughes, and the Methodist member of staff, Ray Billington, were deeply involved in SLIM chaplaincy work. SLIM also represented a major ecumenical undertaking, with members of different denominations accepted on an equality, albeit Anglican led. SLIM's very comprehensive programme of lay training was well ahead of its time. Robinson credited SLIM with having done the only real training of laity in the Diocese until Wychcroft was opened. Cecilia Goodenough's part in it was recognised by the conferring of a Lambeth Doctorate of Divinity by Archbishop Michael Ramsey in 1972.

From the mid 1950's Stockwood had advocated worker priests. There was one worker priest in the diocese in 1960, Ken Ramsay. He had been much influenced by Martyn Grubb and had first worked in Southwark at an engineering works, together with his wife, while living at the vicarage of Peter Duncan. After a short spell driving a van for Unichem, Ramsay then worked for an electronics company, living latterly at St. Andrew's Vicarage, Earlsfield. On Sundays he assisted with services at the churches. He belonged to a group called the Worker Church Group. The group visited worker priests in France and shared experiences. He found Stockwood very supportive and was encouraged to meet with those training on the Southwark Ordination Course. In due course, with the ordination of those training with S.O.C. the number of worker priests considerably increased, so that by 1969 the chapter of worker-priests in Southwark Diocese was some thirty strong, though few if any worked on the shop floor, as Ramsay did. A layperson at Woolwich, Mary Every, lived under rule in the spirit of Charles de Foucauld while she worked at a motorcycle factory. Robinson led a group of clergy and laity from the diocese to visit Pontigny and Taizé in 1967; they too met with worker priests in training at Pontigny.

Stockwood responded to the Arbuthnot Report, on diocesan

boundaries in London and the South-East of England, at his Diocesan Conference in November 1967. Although the Commission had not been allowed to consider the idea of a new province, an Archbishopric of London, co-terminous with Greater London, it was a solution that commended itself to him, indeed he thought that in time to come commonsense would demand its creation. The government of London had been reformed by the London Government Act of 1963 to reduce in number but greatly to increase in size the inner London Boroughs and to include a considerable number of outer London Boroughs, in part from the surrounding counties. His vision was that corresponding to each of the thirty-two boroughs would be a deanery, led by a Borough Dean, perhaps, but not necessarily, a bishop. His policy was to delegate responsibility and he wished to see the deaneries have considerable powers to control their own resources – men, money and buildings. The Borough Deans would represent the Church to the local authority. 'We need a persona in each borough and RDC to lead the Church, to speak for the Church and to organise the Church.' There would also be sub-deaneries, corresponding more with existing rural deaneries. This additional administrative level was not entirely satisfactory. Stockwood's recommendation of a London Province was not taken up, but Borough Deans were indeed appointed (some had been already) and have continued. Borough Deans, together with Sub-Deans and Rural Deans, were in fact elected, an innovation on Stockwood's part. The first such (to Stockwood's surprise) was Stacey, Borough Dean of Greenwich; Lewisham followed soon after electing Allan Auckland; the first full time Borough Dean was John Southgate, Stacey's successor in the Borough of Greenwich. Earlier in 1967 Stockwood had called in a management consultant, Edwin Smith, the Management Development Adviser to the Industrial Society. His brief was to look at 'Management by Objectives' for the diocese. The project raised questions of management structure, objectives and accountability in church life (it seemed to strengthen the case for borough deans), but it also aroused a good deal of resistance among the clergy. It was thus only considerably later (in 1986/7) that a regular pattern of interviews for the clergy with assessment of objectives was introduced.

Southwark Cathedral was by no means isolated from the ferment in the diocese, and indeed made a considerable contribution to it. Ernest Southcott had been appointed Provost in 1961, moving from being Vicar of Halton, Leeds; he succeeded George Reindorp. The appointment was the Crown's, but Stockwood very much wanted him. The canons included Gordon Davies, who was a member of the Chapter when Stockwood was appointed, Stanley Evans, appointed 1960, Frank Colquhoun, 1961, Douglas Rhymes, 1962, Derek Tasker 1962, John Pearce-Higgins, 1963, and after Evans' death, Eric James, 1966. Southcott soon transferred the location of the Sunday morning eucharist from the high altar to the crossing beneath the tower (a location which had been used at ordinations since as long before as 1954). Representative clergy from the diocese would concelebrate and laymen and laywomen read lessons and lead intercessions. The Peace was shared (a little more formally than has become common) throughout the congregation. In 1968 a report on the cathedral was commissioned from the Institute for the Study of Worship and Religious Architecture of the University of Birmingham. In it there is an extended essay by Southcott, which provides a vivid picture of the life of the Cathedral at that time and of his hopes for its future. Southcott's vision was of a multipurpose building, for great liturgical occasions, for diocesan gatherings, for Sunday nights at Southwark, for plays and concerts, for smaller meetings, discussion groups, lectures, Council and Cathedral Parish meetings. Sunday nights at Southwark, very much Southcott's own initiative, was an open forum which dealt with subjects which varied from drug addiction to the arts in education, from sport to music. One series was on the disabled. Sessions on

Sunday evenings and Wednesday lunchtimes showed the problems of the physically handicapped, including the deaf and the blind, as well as the mentally handicapped, including the autistic, both children and adults. Speakers included the parents of a mentally handicapped child, the wife of a man who was mentally ill, a deaf and dumb participant, using an interpreter, doctors, social workers and a representative of a voluntary organisation. In another series the testimony of a recovered alcoholic evoked warm applause. The meetings attracted as many as 600 people. Light refreshments and wine were served by way of hospitality after the talks – a controversial thing to do at that time. Southcott hoped the cathedral would be a centre for training for a wide variety of caring professions as well as church people, P.C.C. members and churchwardens. The Southwark Ordination Course used it weekly on Thursdays for their Communion before a lecture in the Chapter House, and the junior clergy used it for post ordination training. The Cathedral was outward looking. A sign-in on world poverty was arranged which 2,750 people signed, including the diocesan bishop; a huge Christmas card was delivered to 10 Downing Street. The Cathedral sponsored notable series of Garbett lectures in the Chapter House, with lecturers including Herbert Butterfield, Joost de Blank and Howard Root. In November 1968 a series of four dialogue sermons was held, with the founder of Alcoholics Anonymous, Gordon Moody; with Kenneth Solly, of the National Society for Mentally Handicapped Children; and with the songwriters Sydney Carter and Donald Swann. With regard to building development Southcott was cautious. He considered it immoral to spend ¼ million pounds on a building next to the Cathedral as a mission and lecture hall.

His expectations for the Cathedral in the year 2001 are remarkable.

We can imagine it with access to the river, with suitable car parks adjacent, with a restaurant and some sort of community centre attached, with residential conference facilities and so on. Meanwhile, I certainly look forward to all kinds of changes at Southwark. For instance I look forward to the time when we shall have an orchestra in the north transept and men and women in a choir at the west end as well as the choir of men and boys in the chancel. We are delighted to have women reading the epistle and gospel in the Cathedral [an unheard of thing at that time]. I very much hope that the first woman to be ordained in the Church of England will be ordained in Southwark Cathedral and I hope it will be when I am still Provost. (And if women priests, why not women servers and stewards!) [11]

Southcott's vision went beyond the Cathedral. He looked forward, for instance, to the rebuilding of the Globe Theatre. It is suggested that the appointment of Southcott as Provost was a misjudgement and indeed the stresses of running the Cathedral did prove too much for him. Nonetheless his imaginative introductions and his vision for the future of a great church deserve acknowledgement.

Children's work underwent a major development under the leadership of Margaret Turk, the Diocesan Adviser. Already there was beginning to be a marked change of attitude so that children were not simply regarded as the church of the future, but as a part of the contemporary church. It was a feature of the liturgical movement that families came to church together, so that Sunday Schools, or Children's Church, were no longer held in the afternoon, but in the morning, at the same time as the parish communion. Stockwood permitted children who were not confirmed to receive Holy Communion. There was an understanding that they would share in the life of continuing groups until they came to Confirmation. Just as important as liturgical change was a change in the style of teaching, such that both children and teachers were regarded as part of a learning community, and that children learned by experience as much as by instruction. Margaret Turk was a member of a group, the Wadderton Group, which, under the inspiration of Colin Alves, produced a series of courses of experiential learning for children from nursery age to secondary school, under the title *Alive in God's World*. It was influential and much used. Cecilia Goodenough was also involved in work with children, particularly disadvantaged children, for whom she had great sympathy and understanding. Youth work, under the leadership of Gwen Rymer, also took a turn to the experiential, so that confirmation preparation might be conducted in cell groups and include visits to other churches or a synagogue. There might also be talks from a teacher, a police officer and a probation officer about their faith. Youth clubs flourished; hundreds of young people would meet in a club each week.

It was only four months before Robinson left the diocese that David Diamond came to it, from a curacy in Liverpool. He and his colleagues at St. Paul's, Deptford, had a very different priestly style from those at Woolwich and Bermondsey, a style which looked back to the Ritualist clergy of the last century, especially to Father Mackonochie ministering at the Dockland parish of St. George in the East and the slum parish of St. Alban, Holborn, where there was devoted pastoral work. Not that St. Paul's Deptford could be dismissed as merely archaic; it was rooted in the contemporary community. If anywhere could give the lie to Stacey's judgment that a working class parish could no longer come alive in the traditional way it would be here.

On the morning of his last day as Bishop of Woolwich Robinson ordained new deacons and priests in Woolwich Parish Church. In the evening there was a celebration of the years in Southwark at the Church of the Ascension, Blackheath, where Paul Oestreicher was Vicar. He had been appointed Director of Lay Training in the diocese earlier in the year, having previously been a curate to Stanley Evans, on the staff of the BBC and Associate Secretary of the International Department at the British

Council of Churches. At the farewell gathering there was given the first performance of *Requiem for the Living* which Cecil Day Lewis had written in 1962 and which Robinson had persuaded Donald Swann to set to music. Sydney Carter read new poetry.

1. Mervyn Stockwood *Cambridge Sermons* 1961 pp 134f
2. Lambeth Palace Library Fisher Papers vol 232 ff 241ff
3. Michael De-la-Noy *Mervyn Stockwood A Lonely Life* 1996 p 108
4. *Over the Bridge* June 1959 pp 91ff
5. *Evening Standard* 9th April 1963
6. *The Observer Colour Supplement* December 6th 1964
7. *The Observer* May 23rd 1965
8. Lambeth Palace Library Ramsey Papers vol 102 f 155
9. *Prism* February 1964 pp 20f
10. Lambeth Palace Library Ramsey Papers vol 102 f 155
11. The Institute for the Study of Worship and Religious Architecture of the University of Birmingham *Cathedral and mission* p 95

3

A New Theology

Even in his first sermon after his appointment, still at Cambridge, looking forward to his ministry at Southwark, Mervyn Stockwood spoke of the necessity to express Christian doctrine in meaningful language, which involved taking into account contemporary thinking. He had this conviction put to the test.

On 19th March 1963 John Robinson's *Honest to God* was published. It was preceded by an article in *The Observer* two days before under the title *Our Image of God Must Go*. Robinson was already well known thanks to the *Lady Chatterley's Lover* case. The article began with an exposition of Bonhoeffer's belief in Christianity without religion and then summarised some of the arguments of the book concerning theism and Christology. The article, together with Robinson's reputation, captured instant attention and played a big part in ensuring that the book sold as it did.

The gestation of *Honest to God* was not sudden. A colleague who had shared in discussions with Robinson at Clare wrote that when he read it, it was very familiar. Robinson himself wrote that it was an attempt to come to terms with convictions gathering in his mind over a number of years, 'a book I long wanted to write.' He had read a sermon by Paul Tillich to students at Wells Theological College as early as 1949. Yet he also insisted that the position he took was almost entirely borne in upon him by his experience since he left the University. It simply could not have been written by him, at any rate, in Cambridge. It was the fruit of Southwark. In spite of its catchy title, it was not primarily an exercise in theological soul-searching. The book was plainly felt, and the section on prayer was strongly personal. Nevertheless it is to fail to do justice to its argument to see it merely as a baring of the theological soul. Nor was it primarily about images of God, as the title of the article in *The Observer* suggested, a suggestion reinforced by the booklet published in reply by Archbishop Michael Ramsey, *Image Old and New*. Certainly it had discussion of images, of height, and depth, up there and out there, of 'an old man in the sky'; but the discussion went beyond merely exchanging one image for another, and they were not regarded as interchangeable. Nor again was it primarily an exposition of the three Teutonic theologians, Dietrich Bonhoeffer, Rudolf Bultmann and Paul Tillich. He did indeed make free use of Bonhoeffer and his 'religionless Christianity'; of Tillich's 'depth and ground of our being'; and Bultmann's 'demythologising'. Robinson did indeed quote them extensively; nevertheless the book was not just a pastiche. It was his own.

At the core of *Honest to God* was a sustained interpretation of the central truth of Christianity in a loosely Hegelian framework borrowed from Tillich, a synthesis of supranaturalism and naturalism. So in relation to the understanding of God, Robinson denied supranaturalism, God 'out there', as he also denied naturalism, 'that God is merely a redundant name for nature or humanity'. The synthesis was that 'God, the unconditional, is to be found only in, with *and under* the conditioned relationships of this life: for he is their depth and significance.' So too in relation to the understanding of Christ, he denied supranaturalism, that Christ was a divine visitant from 'out there'; and naturalism, that Jesus was 'the most God-like man that ever lived', but no more. The synthesis was that 'in the man Christ Jesus stands revealed, exposed at the surface level of "flesh", the depth and ground of all our being as Love. The life of God, the ultimate Word of Love in which all things cohere, is bodied forth completely, unconditionally and without reserve in the life of a man – the man for others and the man for God.' The same pattern was applied to ethics. He denied supranaturalism, that 'the commandments which God gives, the laws which he lays down ... come down direct from heaven, and are eternally valid

43

for human conduct.' Ethical naturalism on the other hand meant that 'any objective or unconditional standard has disappeared in a morass of relativism and subjectivism.' The synthesis was simple but profound, recognizing 'as the basis of every relationship and every decision, the unconditional love of Jesus Christ, "the man for others".'

A further theme was the 'personality' of God. He pointed out that classical Christian theology had not spoken of God as 'a person', partly because the term was already pre-empted for the three 'persons' of the Trinity. Yet he held that theism as it was ordinarily conceived understood by a personal God a supreme Person, a self existent subject of infinite goodness and power, who entered into a relationship with us comparable with that of one human personality with another. Such a view he neither wished to endorse or deny. Rather would he say that 'God is personal' is to say that 'reality at its very deepest level is personal' or that 'statements about God are statements about the "ultimacy" of personal relationships'. 'Belief in God is the trust, the well nigh incredible trust, that to give ourselves to the uttermost in love is not to be confounded but to be accepted, that Love is the ground of our being, to which we ultimately "come home".'

Robinson was accused of abandoning faith in God by both the 'orthodox' and self-confessed atheists. Apart from his own clear declaration that he had not, appreciation of his aim of reaching a resolution between supranaturalism and naturalism would have made his intention clear. Of the reviewers of the book included in *The Honest to God Debate* only Bultmann seems to have appreciated this point. Interwoven with the Tillichian argument was Bonhoeffer's plea for 'religionless' Christianity. Robinson pilloried the writer who asked 'What can be done to make the church more religious?.. Certainly something must be done...we must... increase our emphasis on the church as a religious organization.' This was symptomatic of South Bank Religion. It was not religionless, but it was highly critical of religion.

Secular Christianity was one of the key themes of the sixties; the sanctuary and emphasis on religious practice were highly suspect. True Christianity belonged in the secular world.

Honest to God was a brilliant book. It had to be read, and countless thousands did read it all over the world. It was also a provoking book (which Robinson foresaw). It evoked a huge correspondence and Robinson received over four thousand letters, to most of which he replied. Many letters were more a matter of feeling than understanding. Some had found the book deeply hurtful; others (including clergy) read it with a sense of relief, even akin to a conversion experience. For many *Honest to God* came to be regarded as a permissive book, not primarily in the sense of moral permissiveness, but rather permissiveness of belief. In the Diocese of Southwark there was both criticism and welcome. One of Robinson's priests wrote:-

In this parish, which I suppose could be called an average country town parish, I doubt if 1 per cent of the population would read or could understand your book; but I expect 20 per cent or so read the article in the *Observer*. Have you thought or considered what a somewhat sceptically-minded person (not a scholar) who had briefly glanced through this article, would say? 'Well, I've always said it's difficult to believe in a God who allows all this suffering and misery that goes on in the world – and now, see – a bishop tells us we needn't believe in God at all – nor go to church. He says religion isn't necessary – it's all phoney; all we need to do is lead decent lives and be kind to others.' Now I know that you did *not* say that, but it is what some have imagined you said in your article. If there are any Christians who really picture God as 'the old man up in the sky', or who imagine that the astronaut is nearer to God than the humble person kneeling at prayer in his own room, they would hardly be of the intelligence required to understand one page of your book. It would not do this if people were to read it very carefully, but I deplore that newspaper article most deeply. You do not make the task of your clergy easier, and I, as a much older man than you, would beg you not to publish these sensational advanced ideas in the public press; for you are not there speaking to trained minds, but to people who need – not the strong meat of the advanced theologian, but the simple milk of the Gospel. We must blend discretion with honesty.[1]

On the other hand Max Warren, the General Secretary of the Church Missionary Society, reviewing the book for the Southwark Diocesan magazine *The Bridge*, was sympathetic:

First let it be said, this is an honest book. Dr Robinson, as we have learnt to expect, looks fearlessly at the real problems which the thoughtful man has about all religion, and about the Christian religion in particular. He also looks quite fearlessly at our Christian vocabulary, and asks whether that vocabulary is good enough. It may be all right as a sort of religious shorthand for use among those who accept the Christian Faith. But can it be used to commend Jesus Christ to those who don't know our shorthand? That is an honest question. It calls for an honest answer by the reader. Dr.Robinson burkes none of the difficulties. Then let it be said, this is a *gentle* book. That may seem a curious adjective to use about one of the hardest hitting books the reader is likely to have met. Yet Dr. Robinson remains all the time very gentle, very sensitive not only to those whom he is trying to reach but also to those Christians who will find his approach very disconcerting and puzzling, and who will not be able to follow him. For all that it is very powerful writing this is not a dogmatic book. All through it the reader will recognize that Dr. Robinson is asking himself questions. He is an explorer. Finally let it be added, the book is fairly tough going. If you take it to bed with you it will either send you off to sleep in five minutes or keep you awake all night! It is that kind of book. But honest to goodness it is worth reading.[2]

Warren was more sympathetic to the author than to puzzled readers in calling *Honest to God* a gentle book. In spite of disclaimers Robinson knew it was provocative, though it must be said that it was never his manner to be deliberately polemical.

The trainee deaconesses at Gilmour House, Clapham, of which the head was Ann Gurney, greeted *Honest to God* more with relief than alarm. They were, though, more sophisticated than might perhaps have been supposed. While he was writing the book, in order to work uninterrupted by the telephone, Robinson used to go to the Diocesan House on Blackheath which formed the centre for the Greyladies community, including some deaconesses, it being near his own home. He would come up once a week, preside at the eucharist and read a fresh chapter to the community. The readings provoked much discussion but were generally very well received. The Senior Chaplain of the South London Industrial Mission, Robert Gibson, found the publication of *Honest to God* a means of opening many doors, which had previously been closed, and of entering a meaningful debate about the Faith with those who had written it off as having little to say to the modern world.

It was different with the evangelical clergy, who condemned it outright; though there certainly were exceptions. There were some 100 evangelical parishes in the diocese out of about 350. When Robinson went to visit clergy chapters he was much attacked. A caring and thoughtful Sunday School superintendent felt that the rug had been pulled out from under her feet. At Richmond the book stirred up enormous interest in the town – most of it aggressively hostile. A number of people wrote to Stockwood demanding that Robinson be unfrocked, and others wrote letters to the press. In view of the fact that a number of regular worshippers were genuinely disturbed by the ideas put forward in the book, the Vicar of Richmond, Derek Landreth, arranged a meeting at the Vicarage to discuss it. So many turned up that they had to move to a hall, and a weekly study group came into being. The end result was that many people found themselves immensely liberated, and fourteen adults offered for confirmation. Robinson himself officiated at the service.

Some churches in the diocese warned the Diocesan Bishop, Stockwood, that if he sent the Bishop of Woolwich to take their confirmation services they would stop their financial dues to the diocese and withdraw their candidates. Some did. The joint secretaries of the Diocesan Conference resigned, and members of the Diocesan Evangelical Clergy Association protested, but the Rural Deans came to the Bishop's support in a letter to *The Times* which read:

> Sir – We have read your report on the Diocese of Southwark, quoted from the *Church Times*, in which a member of the Greater Chapter declares that "the diocese is seething because of present trends". We believe that this is a dangerously misleading statement. As Rural Deans we are in close touch with the clergy of our deaneries and we believe that the great majority are wholeheartedly behind the Bishop of Southwark in his aims and approach.'[3]

Most rural deans signed.

The reaction of the Archbishop of Canterbury, Michael Ramsey, was at first highly critical. Very shortly after the book's publication he said on television that the book caricatured the ordinary Christian's view of God. 'It is utterly wrong and misleading to denounce the imagery of God held by Christian men, women and children: imagery that they have got from Jesus himself, the image of God the Father in Heaven, and to say that we can't have any new thought until it is all swept away.' The reaction of Stockwood was thus crucial. Robinson had given Stockwood the script of *Honest to God* before publication and he had read it with sympathetic interest, yet without full understanding; he had set himself to read it three times. He seems to have seen the issues to be those of language, not of concept, yet recognised that it differed from his own theological views, which were liberal, not radical. Nevertheless a quotation from his *The Faith Today* shows a remarkable resemblance to Robinson's thought: 'Jesus knew that the kingdom would never be furthered like that [fantasies of the supernatural] but by the reverse, by finding the supernatural in the natural.' Stockwood may have suggested alterations which were incorporated in the finished book, but probably did not; certainly no formal episcopal approval was either sought or given. He did not foresee the reaction to the book. Not long after publication Stockwood found himself deluged by hostile letters; there was even pressure for proceedings for heresy in the consistory court. Stockwood was considerably distressed by this opposition – he did not mind fighting his own battles, but was less keen on fighting other people's – and he found himself in the position of having to defend a book he did not wholly understand against his Metropolitan, Ramsey, who was a more learned theological scholar than he, and also a host of other critics. He was a little slow to declare himself and delayed his response for three weeks after publication. He took his stance publicly in an article in the *Evening Standard* under the title 'Should Dr. Robinson have written that book?' His defence of Robinson was on three grounds. One was an appeal to the tradition of theological liberalism, represented by former scholars such as F.D. Maurice, Charles Gore and William Temple, who had been innovators but who had come to be greatly respected in the Church. Another was his knowledge of Robinson and his respect for his integrity and devotion. The third was the appreciation of Robinson's missionary, outgoing purpose. Stockwood declared what he had said more than once before – his openness to the contemporary expression of the faith.

At the end of the month Stockwood wrote to Ramsey:

As the Bishop of Woolwich works in my diocese two points occur to me. If you state publicly that the doctrines of God and the deity of Christ in Robinson's book are incompatible with the doctrine of the Church, it is possible that pressure will be brought to bear upon me to take action against the Bishop. If this were to happen I should have to make up my mind about what action, if any, to take. I have and am consulting theologians but there is a division of opinion. I shall, of course, treat your verdict with the utmost respect but until it has been carefully considered by our best theological minds, I cannot at this stage commit myself. It is my hope that a situation will not develop which might lead to estrangement between my Diocese and the Province with the possibility of the Archbishop and the Diocesan Bishop on different sides, and perhaps in open conflict. So far as my Diocese is concerned I am striving to bring the different parties together to talk over their viewpoints. I am refraining from saying anything that might be interpreted as an official pronouncement because it would hinder constructive discussion and encourage men to harden their attitudes. Although bishops have been receiving many letters of protest from the critics, we must not be allowed to forget the people on the other side who have not written. My guess is there will be a reaction, perhaps a strong one, in favour of the Bishop of Woolwich. This could be disastrous as it might lead to the sort of situation that existed a hundred years ago at the time of *Essays and Reviews* when the book was condemned synodically in Convocation, when eleven thousand clergymen declared their hostility to the doctrines it expressed and when only three bishops were willing to take part in Frederick Temple's consecration. No doubt we shall be more circumspect today, but the cleavage might be as serious.[4]

The Archbishop spoke on *Honest to God* in Convocation early in May. Though he was critical, the criticism was measured. He did say, 'I doubt whether any argument could show that the doctrine which so far emerges is properly the same as the doctrine of the church.' But no official action was ever taken. Much later Ramsey wrote to Stockwood that his initial reaction was very harsh and very unsympathetic and 'over-reacting'. He soon came to see the matter differently and blamed himself for his initial attitude.

Within days of the publication date Robinson was responding to invitations to talk to groups in the diocese in parishes and elsewhere. Two early ones were meetings with sixth formers at St. Dunstan's College, Catford, in his episcopal area. Then in June he went to the Froebel Institute at Roehampton for a meeting of the entire college, staff and students in the hall. There were many more. Robinson and his wife held a series of conferences at Wychcroft, the Southwark Diocesan training centre, to follow up *Honest to God*. He called them 'Hooks and Eyes' conferences:

> Just before Easter 1964 I invited to a week-end at our diocesan training centre a group of some of the many people who had written to me over the past year. They represented a cross-section of those to whom the Church as it at present exists appears to have no hooks for their eyes. They were either 'insiders' hanging on because to come out would have seemed the greater betrayal, or 'outsiders' who would have liked to be in but felt that to do so would have meant denying too much in themselves which they knew to be true. Or they were Christians who had given up more than occasional church services because they knew their limitations and found that their faith, hope and charity were just not strong enough!'.[5]

The group was highly critical and stimulating. From it emerged two things which for Robinson were to some extent a surprise. The first was the vehemence with which almost everyone reacted against the traditional credal and liturgical formulae. The second was the demand that not only must the Church's theology be open-ended, it must itself be a genuinely open society, an 'accepting community'. A further surprise was that the highlight of the week-end proved to be the Sunday service to which Robinson was already committed – a celebration of Baptism, Confirmation and Communion restored, as in the early Church, to a single liturgical whole. It showed that the traditional liturgy of the Church well and imaginatively done still had the power to provide hooks for people's eyes.

There were clergy in the diocese for whom formal subscription to the Thirty-Nine Articles of Religion caused difficulty. For the meeting of Diocesan Conference in November 1962 Walter Matthews, the Dean of St. Paul's, had been invited to speak and he advocated reform. The academically brilliant Nick Earle, a former curate of Stockwood, had already felt unable to accept preferment because of the necessity to assent. John Pearce-Higgins, who had an equally distinguished academic record and who was Chairman of the Modern Churchmen's Union, and whom Stockwood appointed Vice-Provost of the Cathedral, also found difficulty. On making his general assent to the Articles he said 'This I shall do in accordance with the law'. He added a statement: 'I protest against the duty and necessity thus imposed upon me. I firmly hold to the Catholic faith as contained in the Creeds and in the Holy Scriptures; but I question the value of the particular interpretation of the faith contained in some of the Articles.' Pearce-Higgins quoted Cyril Garbett, a former Bishop of Southwark, who had not been happy with the Articles as a standard of doctrinal orthodoxy. Pearce-Higgins continued that the Articles were a Reformation document, originally set out in all sincerity within the limitations of thought and under the stress of the theological and social pressures of the time, and reflecting the views of the Church of England four hundred years ago. They appeared to him to be in the nature of a theological fossil embedded in the constitution of the Church of England. Many years had passed since Dr. Garbett's words were delivered to the ordinands of the diocese, and yet nothing had been done to free the clergy from the necessity of assent. Hence his protest. He hoped it, with the strong feeling already expressed in many quarters, would lead to the abolition of assent as a condition of office. Pearce-Higgins received a considerable correspondence as a result of his statement, including one letter signed by two-thirds of the students at one of the larger theological colleges supporting his protest. The evangelical clergy were deeply hostile, as on the one hand the Thirty-Nine Articles were adhered to as an essential definition of Protestant faith and on the other Pearce-Higgins' interest in the paranormal (he was Vice-Chairman of the Churches Fellowship for Psychical and Spiritual Studies) aroused deep suspicion. The issue aroused much stronger feelings than *Honest to God*. A little later Stockwood wrote to Ramsey sharing his concern over subscription to the Articles; this led, in due course, to the setting up of a new Doctrine Commission and a greatly modified form of assent.

By the middle of 1964 there was considerable talk of a new Reformation. So Robinson's next book was *The New Reformation?* He prudently added a question mark, though it tended to disappear as the book progressed. In it he took up the secular, worldly concerns of *Honest to God*. Theology had to start from the gracious neighbour, rather than the gracious God. The inductive approach to Christian doctrine began with Jesus as *completely* human, the Man for others. The church was the accepting community. No longer could it be anti-humanist doctrinally or morally. 'Unless the Church can really convince men that it is more deeply and honestly interested in persons for their own sake than any of the other humanisms of our day, then I believe it will merely be judged by them – and the standard of judgment will be that of the Son of Man.' Robinson put forward an interesting programme for contemporary theological study with all the material from the twentieth century – Twentieth Century Church History, A Twentieth Century Theology of Mission, Contemporary Systematic Theology and Contemporary Ethics. Tellingly he ended his book with one of the most enigmatic passages of scripture "'Watchman, what of the night? Watchman, what of the night?' The watchman says: 'Morning comes, and also the night.If you will inquire, inquire; come back again.'" (Isaiah 21.11-12), questioning what was to come. 'Is the church *free* enough to be there, to let itself "take shape around [Christ's] servant presence in the world?" That is the crucial question for the new Reformation.' He was optimistic. 'There is plenty even within the diocese I serve to show that from [the traditional parochial structures of the Church] too ensigns of hope can be set up – so that "Southwark" has become not only a by-word but a sign for many.'[6] The book was too slight greatly to advance the movement that had started, but it had value in 'grounding' the ideas of *Honest to God*.

John Robinson had *But that I can't believe*! published in the same year. In spite of its title the book consists more in exposition of revised belief than disbelief. Many of its short pieces were written for a mass circulation readership. It is evident that this was not a milieu in which he was at ease; indeed he himself implied it. Simplifications and shortenings sometimes make him appear an old style Modernist. There was an article on the Holy Spirit, not previously published, convincingly correcting the impression that *Honest to God* had nothing to say about the Spirit. 'The whole book was about the Spirit – and people did not recognize it. For the Spirit is pre-eminently the aspect of the reality of God I was trying to bring home. He is the very ground of our being, nearer to us than our own selves, the beyond *in the midst*.' The weakest article was that on the Trinity, which Robinson had difficulty regarding as more than a formula.

A much more substantial book was *Exploration into God*. Where *Honest to God* was provocative this book was considered and reflective. Robinson said that he felt perhaps that he put more of himself into it than any other. There is a chapter on the 'death of God' controversy, associated with the American writers William Hamilton and Thomas Altizer, which Robinson perceptively reckoned might be transient. It ended with a stout defence of God-language. In the chapter *Locating the reality of God* he considers Paul van Buren's *Secular Meaning of the Gospel*, which is expressed without 'supra-sensible metaphysical entities', e.g.'if love for the neighbour is the test of "love for God", then by the verification principle it is the meaning of "love for God".' Van Buren gets along without using the word God. In response Robinson gives meaning to it not 'metaphysically', but with a strongly existentialist understanding. 'Through this event or person there meets me a claim, a mystery, a grace, whose overriding, transcendent, unconditional character can only be expressed by responding, with the prophet, "Thus saith the Lord".' At the core of the book Robinson contrasts the 'secularizers' including Bonhoeffer, van Buren and Harvey Cox, with the more philosophical or mystical Tillich, Teilhard de Chardin, Buber and Nicolas Berdyaev. He notes four points of convergence between them all. Firstly, that a dualistic model of the universe is out. 'The traditional divisions with which theology has worked – body and soul, earth and heaven, this world and the other world, the secular and the sacred, the two natures human and divine, and so forth – are decreasingly viable or useful'. Secondly, the implication of this is not the abolition of the transcendent in pure naturalism; it is the apprehension of the transcendent as given in, with and under the immanent. Thirdly there is a marked reticence in speaking of God, both in the secularizing tradition, which insists that nothing can be said of God apart from personal relationships, and in the mystical, philosophical tradition where it is expressed by apophatic theology. The fourth point is that the old division between theist and atheist had become much less sharp. He quotes Michael Novak, 'Many a believer feels out of step with others in his generation. He neither believes with the believers, nor disbelieves with the atheists. These considerations lead Robinson to panentheism, defined as 'the belief that the Being of God includes and penetrates the whole universe, so that every part of it exists in him, but (as against pantheism) that his Being is more than, and is not exhausted by, the universe'. He goes on to consider the doctrine of creation. He rejects the image of the potter and the pot as sub-personal, and proposes instead evocation, so that the the whole universe evolves or better is called out from the lifeless to the biological, but sub-personal, and then to the level of personality. Divine Providence is not to be expressed in terms of a Planner and Purposer, who fits each effect to its cause to accomplish his grand design, but that 'for those who make the response of love, in every concatenation of circumstance, however pointless and indeed intention-less, there is to be met the graciousness of a "Thou" capable of transforming and liberating even the most baffling and opaque into meaning and purpose.' And again, 'There is no aspect of nature or history, however resistant to personal categories, that is not *ultimately* to be seen in terms of spirit, freedom, love. From the start, affirms the believer, this is a "personalizing" universe, in the sense that the whole is to be understood as a process making for personality and beyond.' This leads him on to evil. He rejects 'a Being who is "personally responsible" for directing the course of events so as to produce the distribution of suffering we see, or even "visiting" individuals with occurences in which they should be able to detect "the hand of God". God is in everything and not merely the obviously good and meaningful, in the cancer, as in the sunset. Panentheism takes its stand against the dualism of theism, moral as well as metaphysical. But it does not side with the indifferentism of pantheism. The evil in the world is not without purpose. The evil in the world is terrifyingly real, both at the sub-personal and at the personal level, but it is still part of the face of *God*.

Robinson concluded:

"God" is not to be understood as an Ego over against the world, a Spirit in contrast with created matter. Rather, if again we are to go on using the word, it must relate to that which compels us to speak of the whole of reality in terms of personal spirit, the transcendent source and goal of all being – in all things and through all things and above all things.'[7]

1. John A.T. Robinson and David L. Edwards *The Honest to God Debate 1963* p 50
2. Ibid pp 90f
3. *The Times* July 3rd 1963
4. Eric James (ed) *A Life of Bishop John A.T. Robinson* 1987 pp 119ff
5. John A.T. Robinson *The New Reformation?* 1965 p 38
6. Ibid p 104
7. John A.T. Robinson *Exploration into God* 1967 p 144

A New Liturgy and Spirituality

At his first Diocesan Conference in June 1959 Mervyn Stockwood opened the way for a degree of liturgical change. He found no fewer than 21 different liturgical uses when he came to the diocese, including the Roman Missal, the liturgy of Taizé and the United Church of South India. So he insisted that the Prayer Book services must be adhered to, but beyond them other ways might be tried out. He said that provided the statutory services were held on Sundays and weekdays he was ready to allow some liturgical experiments to be made and indeed he hoped to have eventually one church in the diocese which would become a liturgical centre, for others to learn from. This latter did not come to pass, but the experiments did, and were fruitful.

Liturgical reform was becoming a widespread concern in the 1960's. Churches with parish communions were still rare when Robinson came to the diocese. By the time he left they were common, except in certain evangelical churches. Often accompanying the parish communion was the adoption of the westward position by the celebrant. Liturgy was one of the particular concerns of Eric James. He had been Chaplain at Trinity College Cambridge and had been appointed Vicar of St. George's Church, Camberwell and Warden of the Trinity College Mission in 1959. In 1965 he became Director of Parish and People and, while continuing to hold that post, next year Canon Precentor at Southwark Cathedral, with special concern for the river-side and inner city parishes in the Diocese. In 1962 he wrote a Prism Pamphlet on *The Roots of the Liturgy*. In it he insisted on the relationship of life in the church to life in society. He commended house churches – the breaking down of large impersonal communities into more personal groups.

Stockwood advocated the use of modern translations of the

Bible. When he ordained a deacon he gave him a copy of *The New Testament in Modern English* by J.B. Phillips. *The New English Bible* New Testament (of which Robinson was a translator) was published in March 1961 and was officially authorised for use for the readings of Holy Communion in 1963. This use of modern language stimulated the demand for modern language liturgy. Stockwood told his clergy he wanted to encourage reasonable experiment in liturgy. He had himself served for a number of years on the Church of England Liturgical Commission and when at St. Matthew, Moorfields, had produced his own revised Baptism service. The Commission had published conservative proposals for baptism and confirmation in 1959, retaining traditional language and style (there was, for instance, much psalmody in the service of infant baptism). The Commission's work was not accepted and there remained a demand, mainly for pastoral reasons, for a much more radical revision, using contemporary language. James published an experimental liturgy for the baptism of infants written by a group of clergy in North Camberwell. As well as abandoning 17th century language it showed commendable simplicity and directness. Two extracts, one from the introduction and one the congregation's response after the baptism, show its style:

> By Baptism a child is made a member of the Church, the Body of Christ.
> Baptism proclaims what Christ in his love has declared: that we are children of God and inheritors of the Kingdom of Heaven. The water of Baptism speaks to us of God's readiness to cleanse us from our sins; of the forgiveness of God that all who respond to His Spirit receive. But there is no magic about Baptism. We must ensure that those who are baptised come to understand what our Lord does for them in this sacrament. They will depend greatly on their parents, who having themselves been baptised are already members of the Church, and especially on the Church where they are brought up.

We receive this child into the congregation of Christ's flock, and we ask for the grace of God, that by love, by prayer and example, we may show *him* true Christian fellowship.'[1]

James said that, having used this liturgy, he never wanted to go back to using that of the Book of Common Prayer.

The team led by Nicolas Stacey at Woolwich also introduced baptismal reform. Instead of having small numbers every Sunday afternoon, christenings were held quarterly. Considerable pastoral care was taken in preparation and follow-up and a rehearsal was held on a weekday evening. A film-strip was shown.

> The christening itself was a moving experience. We had completely rewritten the service. Unlike the one in the Prayer Book our christening service was simple and understandable. Each service had all the excitement and expectation of a great occasion. The church was packed and each family had its own pew specially reserved for it. The regular members of our congregation and the choir were present. We had a portable font which we put at the chancel steps. For the first part of the service the mothers and babies sat in the lounge where the service was relayed to them. Then, about a third of the way through, came the first moment of high drama. The mothers came down from the lounge and, proudly holding their babies in their arms, proceeded down the main aisle led by a robed cross bearer, servers and a priest. They stopped opposite the pews where the families were sitting and, still standing in the aisles, they were asked by the priest conducting the service, "What do you in the name of these children ask of the Church of God?", to which the parents replied, "We ask for Baptism." The priest then asked, "Why do you ask for Baptism?", and they replied "That our children may be made Christians."

After each baby was christened we walked up the entire

length of the main aisle holding the baby in our arms as we said the words "Receive the sign of the Cross of Christ in token that thou shalt not be ashamed to confess the faith of Christ crucified and manfully to fight under His banner against sin, the world and the devil and to continue His faithful soldier and servant until thy life's end.".... Finally we got the whole of the congregation to say together, "We receive these children into the congregation of Christ's flock, and we ask for the Grace of God, that by love, by prayer and example we may show them true Christian fellowship as long as they live among us."

Stacey commented, 'I think the parents who had their children christened at St. Mary's felt something important and solemn had happened to their babies.'[2]

Stockwood took up the matter of liturgical reform in his letter in *The Bridge* in May 1964. He had set up a Liturgical Committee under his own chairmanship and it had prepared supplementary services for parish use for Advent, Mothering Sunday and Holy Week. A new service for the Institution of an Incumbent was also prepared. For the Holy Week services Prayer Book idiom was retained (Series III was still a long way off) and the emphasis was on brevity and simplicity. Palm Sunday offered an outdoor procession; Maundy Thursday had the foot washing, the eucharist of the Upper Room and the stripping of the altar. No provision was made for a Maundy Thursday vigil, though some churches who used the services did keep one. The Good Friday Liturgy combined Mattins, the Litany, the Veneration of the Crucified, Holy Communion and Evensong. Provision was also made for the Easter Vigil, with lections, the blessing of the New Fire and lighting of the Paschal Candle, Adult Baptism and Confirmation and/or the re-affirmation of Baptismal Vows, and the Holy Communion. In practice churches varied over holding the Easter Eucharist at midnight or on the morning of Easter Day. In 1963 Stockwood himself presided at the Holy Week ceremonies at St. Peter's, Streatham, while Robinson presided at Holy Trinity, Roehampton. At the end of the year all the clergy of the diocese were asked to attend a demonstration of the liturgies with a commentary by Stockwood in the Church of St. John the Divine, Kennington. Many parishes were introduced to the idea of a corporate liturgical keeping of the week who, without a strong lead from the Bishop would not have considered it at all. The Committee also drafted a new Communion Service; it was not permissible that it be used, but was intended to serve for discussion while the Archbishops' Liturgical Commission prepared an alternative rite. Stockwood stressed that his committee's service proclaimed all the saving acts of God, the Incarnation, the Resurrection, the Ascension and Pentecost as well as Calvary, which alone the Prayer Book spoke of. And the structure and actions of the liturgy, which the Prayer Book interrupted with other matter, were made clear. Series II, when it came, had been prepared for and was widely acceptable in the diocese. Stockwood gave a demonstration of Series II at St. Catherine's, Hatcham.

A full treatment of prayer was provided by Douglas Rhymes in *Prayer in the Secular City*. Rhymes had been Vicar of All Saints, New Eltham until 1962, when he became Canon Librarian at the the Cathedral. He also served as the first Warden of Wychcroft, the Diocesan Training Centre. He drew on the experience of a group of younger priests from the inner city. From his book it is plain that Rhymes had been familiar and at home with traditional patterns of prayer; nevertheless his book is a plea for change, a marrying of the traditional and secular Christianity. *Prayer in the Secular City* was much indebted to Robinson, especially *Honest to God*, with its questioning of God as a separate person and as a being 'out there'. It owed a debt to Harvey Cox's *Secular City* and Paul van Buren's *The Secular Meaning of the Gospel*. It was sympathetic too to existentialism. It showed confidence in the value of groups, under the influence of psychological and other forms of group work. All this was worked out in his treatment of private prayer and corporate prayer. Rhymes' book was in its way very characteristic of South Bank religion.

Robinson's *But that I can't believe* has a chapter on non-liturgical prayer. Michel Quoist's *Prayers of Life* delighted him and he regarded it as classic. The style of prayer starting from life 'just as it comes' accorded very much with his priorities. He mentioned other books, including Malcolm Boyd's *Are you running with me, Jesus?* These prayers by an American Episcopalian priest who had ministered in universities and in civil rights groups had section headings 'Prayers for the Free Self', 'Prayers for the Free Society', 'Prayers in the City', 'Meditations on Films', 'Prayers for Sexual Freedom'; they were both sensitive and powerful. Robinson reckoned that in them what Boyd called 'the heretical gap' between the holy and the profane had quite disappeared. The controlling rubric of such prayer, Robinson judged, might be Dag Hammarskjöld's 'in our era, the road to holiness necessarily passes through the world of action.' God was to be met in, with and under, not apart from, response to the world, the neighbour. Its form of the divine was more often than not the Son of Man incognito. Nevertheless he noted that these prayers had an odd conversational tone, with frequent interjections of 'Lord' or 'Jesus'. 'Does this take the other "Thou" with real seriousness and the fact that the claim of the unconditional must be met *in him* and *through him* – even if it is not possible or natural to say "Lord, Lord"?' Robinson commended the far more reserved Quaker tradition of spirituality, which had its ambience much more in the Spirit and which saw the Presence rather in terms of what lit up every man from within.

In the early 1960's there began to be, amongst some Anglican evangelicals, an interest in Pentecostalism, and some experienced the charismatic renewal of Baptism of the Holy Spirit. It was found in the neighbouring diocese of Rochester at St. Paul's

Beckenham at the end of 1963 and next year reached some evangelicals in Bermondsey, particularly at the Cambridge University Mission, where Michael Whinney gave positive leadership. Not all evangelical leaders were happy about this renewal, however. Stockwood wanted to know about it and was accepting and supportive. In the summer of 1964 he spent a day of prayer, Bible reading and study with three ordained men from the diocese. At the eucharist all three spoke in tongues. Stockwood enabled charismatic Anglicans to remain firmly within the diocese and Anglican tradition by his involving himself both privately and publicly with what was happening. A curate in Rotherhithe, Nicholas Rivett-Carnac, at Holy Trinity Church, experienced baptism in the Spirit through the ministry of Vic Ramsey at Orange Street Congregational Church, a noted charismatic centre. After a rather unsettled career as an army officer and then as a shipbroker, Rivett-Carnac had spent nine months at the Bede House Settlement in Bermondsey working with alienated young people. He trained and worked as a probation officer before offering for ordination and in due course returning to the Borough of Bermondsey as a curate. After some time there he received Ramsey's message of conversion and was baptised in the spirit.

> Nicholas felt as if something had burst within him, a torrent of feelings and longings all poured out in that one, single-syllabled cry in another tongue. For over a hour he cried out in this way. All his stiff-upper-lip reserve melted in the joy and peace that flooded through him. It was like coming home, like the end of a long journey... Shortly after this Nicholas received further prayer and was released into praying fluently in tongues.[3]

Michael Whinney laid hands on him for spiritual renewal. Rivett-Carnac's experience was of importance in itself and also because it led on to a ministry, in the diocese, at St. Mark's Kennington, where he was able to lead many others to share in the same renewal.

A chapter in *Exploration into God* continued Robinson's inquiry into prayer. He himself was a secularist or a prophet rather than a mystic, yet the mystical tradition had a real appeal to him with its 'journey inwards' to the 'deep centre'. For him it had to be a world affirming mysticism, not a world denying mysticism of detachment. 'In spirituality as in theology I find myself returning to the utterly personal panentheism of the God dwelling incognito at the heart of all things.'

In *Christian Freedom in a Permissive Society* Robinson had a wide ranging essay *Meeting, Membership and Ministry* which dealt with matters of Christian initiation. He asked for an alternative service to offer in place of infant Baptism, a service of thanksgiving, naming, blessing and dedication. He held that the theological (and liturgical) norm of Christian initiation was adult Baptism, Confirmation and Communion administered together (his own practice as a bishop). In considering the relationship between baptism, confirmation and communion, nothing should be delayed for non-adults except what it was possible for an adult alone to give or receive. Further everything that belonged to Membership should be given to the Christian as he was incorporated into the Body of Christ at baptism. There was no case for a distinction between membership and full membership, let alone for parcelling out the Spirit by measure (such as was implied in much popular rationale of the Baptism-Confirmation divide). Communicant status and a share in the Spirit-filled community were implied by the very relationship of membership in Christ. With regard to the ministry of Confirmation, that part of the rite as it was then understood which was the completion or closing act of Baptism, should be restored where it belonged, in the baptismal liturgy. The other aspect of Confirmation – all that had come to be seen in it as 'the ordination of the laity' – should be placed where it too belongs, namely, with whatever action or rite is appropriate to give expression to the relationship not of Membership but of Ministry. It would be better called Commissioning. Implied in Robinson's argument is that baptised children should be admitted to communion without any further condition; and also that Confirmation, or Commissioning, should be essentialy a rite for adults.

The liturgical movement also had its effect on church buildings. In his letter in the Diocesan Leaflet for August 1960 Stockwood commended Peter Hammond's *Liturgy and Architecture* and he wrote:

> A church is first and foremost the place where the people of God meet to take part in the Liturgy, and to hear the Scriptures. Hence the Communion Table, instead of being a sideboard at the east wall, should be in a position of prominence so that priest and people can gather around it and it should be visible to the whole congregation. The Bishop, who is president of the Eucharist, should have his throne behind the Table and the presbyters their seats on either side. The approach to the Table should not be cluttered up with choir stalls and prayer desks, because if we are to take our biblical theology seriously the whole congregation should have immediate access to the altar... Fortunately there are still a few churches to be built in the Southwark Diocese and I am asking those responsible for drawing up the plans to arrange joint consultations between architects, theologians and liturgists. As Mr. Hammond says, the task of the architect is not to design a building that looks like a church, but to create a building that works as a place for liturgy. And the first and essential requirement is radical functional analysis.[4]

Robinson shared this concern for church architecture; he supplied the preface to the report of a conference held in May 1961 published as *Making the Building Serve the Liturgy – Studies in the re-ordering of churches*. In it he wrote:

We are now being reminded that the church people go to has an immensely powerful psychological effect on their vision of the Church they are meant to be. The church building is a prime aid, or a prime hindrance, to the building up of the Body of Christ. And what the building says so often shouts something completely contrary to all that we are seeking to express through the liturgy. And the building will always win – unless and until we can make it say something else.[5]

He too commended Hammond's *Liturgy and Architecture*.

At the beginning of the decade churches were being consecrated in which all the seating faced in one direction, from liturgical west to liturgical east, all the furnishings were fixed and in which the altar was placed up against the east wall, necessitating eastward position (westward position was the most widely adopted hallmark of liturgical reform). The movement of space is 'processional' or 'hieratic'. The first church to adopt the principles of the Liturgical Movement was St. Mary, Peckham, rather unexpectedly one from the Evangelical tradition. A brochure was produced shortly after the church was consecrated in 1962 with the principles on which the incumbent, Victor King, and the architects, Robert Potter and Richard Hare, based the design.

We start with a table for it is from the position of the LORD'S TABLE in an Anglican church that the Word is preached and the sacrament is dispensed. In the Holy Communion Service of the Church of England the Word of God is read (Commandments, Epistle and Gospel), and in our new St. Mary's at each celebration there is an exposition of the Word of God. Therefore the LORD'S TABLE is the most important piece of furniture. In our new Church planning the Architects started with the Table. They made it the focal point of the whole building and it is almost the geometric centre... In our new Church the building is subordinated to the will of the people of God who are themselves the Church. It is functional – made to be used, and not primarily to be looked at. Its striking appearance is in no way of prime importance, for of all the false requirements, sometimes demanded by sentimentalists, the requirement that a building must 'look like a Church' is the most false. Each member is part of the whole, and can realise this physically by the close proximity to the LORD'S TABLE. God is known through His Word and through the breaking of the Bread. Everyone is near enough to see and to share in the central acts of consecration. God is in the midst.[6]

In plan the church is in the form of a blunt cross with the Holy Table central and the seating facing it on three sides. The Table, font, pulpit, lectern and clergy seats are all moveable, which allows for flexibility and experimentation in layout. In practice the position of the Table is not easily changed and is a little awkward, as, if the side seating is used, the president does not face all the congregation. The exterior is successful.

The chapel at Wychcroft, the Chapel of the People of God (being a centre for lay training), was also planned in accordance with the principles of the Liturgical Movement. John Hayward worked together with Robinson, placing the freestanding altar centrally to one long wall, while round the other walls was seating. The pulpit stood opposite the altar. Above and behind the altar on the wall stood an imposing icon 'Christ the Worker', also by Hayward. In it the risen Christ, with a short robe and a carpenter's apron extends his hands and his feet with the marks of the nails of crucifixion. He has a halo with a cross to his head. The background to the figure, in a cross shape, is of plain and varnished wood. An aureole is defined by the varnishing of the wood. The icon had, and still has after re-ordering, a strong defining effect on the chapel as a whole.

Other new churches of the decade after 1962 had the central altars of the liturgical movement. An unusually satisfying interior is to be found at St. John, Peckham, by David Bush. The planning was begun with a weekend conference of clergy and parishioners under the guidance of Robinson, in whose episcopal area the church was to lie. The design is one of considerable subtlety. The main worship area is square. The axis to the altar and two blocks of seating, which take up more than half the available space, is off centre to the room as a whole. A third block of seating accommodating an unrobed choir and more members of the congregation faces at right angles to the others towards the side of the altar, effectively creating the feeling of worship 'in the round'. The altar lies well away from the 'east' wall, and is emphasized by a podium. The roof has a two-way pitch and a timber ceiling slopes down steeply above the liturgical area to a richly colourful beton-glass window of the Creation by Susan Johnson. Natural light from a tower feature throws the altar into relief and also highlights a figure of the crucified Christ on the wall behind it. The worship area which has a subdued light leads into a brighter lobby and opposite are glazed doors giving on to a garden courtyard, a highly welcome feature in Peckham.

The most versatile church artist working in the diocese was John Hayward. In addition to the large icon in the chapel at Wychcroft there are windows and a fine iconographic ensemble in Christ Church, Streatham, where he was a parishioner, a very fine window in St. Matthew, Camberwell, and a number of works elsewhere. Hayward's work represented a revived and renewed iconographic tradition.

Church music also had its innovations. The pioneer had been Geoffrey Beaumont, Vicar of St. George, Camberwell till 1959, who had composed his *20th Century Folk Mass* in 1956. He had responded to a fellow vicar who complained that church music was utterly foreign to the majority of church people. Beaumont intended his setting to be 'normal everyday popular type of music'. He effectively used the same popular idiom for new settings to old hymns. *Now thank we all our God* and *Lord, thy word abideth* were much sung. Perhaps in a way their very ephemerality was a tribute to the fulfilment of his intention and his success. Round him came into being the 20th Century Church Light Music Group of which the most notable member was Patrick Appleford, at that time Youth and Education Secretary of SPG and living in Camberwell. His *Mass of Five Melodies* was published in 1961; its intention was that it might prove to be a musical setting of the liturgy which all members of the congregation could sing, avoiding becoming merely another musical setting singable only by the musicians and not by the whole people of God. The Group was clearly influenced by the Liturgical Movement, which taught that the liturgy was the work of the whole church, not merely of the ministers (including in that designation the choir). The intention was to produce music that was congregational and easily singable, and that aim was indeed achieved. Appleford both wrote and set hymns, of which the best known is probably the fine *Lord Jesus Christ*; *Jesus our Lord, our King and our God* is also attractive. Where words and music marry together (these hymns use modern language) the result has the potential to be more long-lasting. The mass settings soon became dated by liturgical change.

In the 1960's Sydney Carter was beginning his very large and deservedly popular output and these years included *Lord of the Dance, Standing in the Rain, When I needed a neighbour* and *Bird of Heaven,* together with with the pointed *I want to have a little bomb like you.* Carter wrote *One more step along the world I go* for a school leavers' service at Southwark Cathedral.

1. *Prism* February 1963 pp 34,36
2. Nicolas Stacey *Who Cares* 1971 pp 147ff
3. Jenny Cooke *Upon this rock* 1989 pp 41f
4. *Southwark Diocesan Leaflet* August 1960. The Bishop's Letter

5. Gilbert Cope (ed) *Making the Building Serve the Liturgy* 1962 p 5
6. Brochure for the Consecration of St. Mary Magdalene, Peckham November 1962

A New Pattern of Ministry

In his enthronement sermon Mervyn Stockwood said:

> From my own experience I know that it is almost impossible to bridge the gulf between the parochial system and the world in which so many people have to live. That is why I should like to see cautious experiments with a new kind of priesthood and a new type of organisation.[1]

Integral to this part of his vision for the diocese was a new type of training for the priesthood. Already in the choosing of a new Bishop of Woolwich he had sought a man who was accustomed to the teaching of ordinands. Curiously, though, he announced at his first Diocesan Conference in June 1959:

> I have appointed the Revd. Eric James, Chaplain of Trinity College, Cambridge, to be Vicar of St. George's Camberwell. He will, I hope, bring with him half a dozen graduates who will earn their living by day in industry and at night will go ahead with their theological studies, and in this connection the new Bishop of Woolwich will be of great assistance. When these men reach ordination level, they may become curates in the ordinary way, or they may feel that they can be of greater use if they remain where they are and discover their way to a new pattern of priesthood. I am fully alive to the dangers of this scheme, but I am prepared to take risks, in order that we shall do something to get alongside that large section of society which has little or nothing to do with the Church.[2]

This was obviously not thought through, not least because James knew that he needed time to address the problems of his new parish. In the event it fell to John Robinson to prepare a scheme based on the Cathedral, which he did with the greatest speed. He drew on his thinking of several years before when he was Chaplain of Wells Theological College. He was able to present a draft for the Southwark Ordination Scheme (as it was first called) to the Bishop's Staff Meeting in January 1960. It was to cater for three types of ordinand – for those who needed to remain in their jobs for family or financial reasons and who were offering for the full time ministry; those working who wished to continue in their jobs after ordination as part time ministers; and younger graduate ordinands who wished to do at least part of their training in the context of the industrial world, whether they intended to work as parish priests, as industrial chaplains or as priest-workers. Academic requirements were outlined. Any serious lowering of standards was regarded as undesirable and the proposals were not to be regarded as ordination on the cheap or by the back door. It was expected that ordinands would need to be trained for a type of spirituality more adapted to life 'in the world' than that which a residential theological college normally presupposed. It was concretely proposed that in September 1960 lectures would be started at the Cathedral Chapter House under the auspices of the London University Extension Board, building on the series of lectures already held there. The three year course would be :

First year	(i)	Old Testament	(24 lectures)
	(ii)	Religious Life and Thought since 1800	(24 lectures)
Second year	(iii)	New Testament	(24 lectures)
	(iv)	Christian Doctrine	(24 lectures)
Third year	(v)	Biblical Theology	(24 lectures)
	(vi)	Liturgy	(12 lectures)
	(vii)	Apologetics	(12 lectures)

It was regarded as important that all through their training the ordinands should meet together and know themselves as a dedicated group under a common discipline and rule of life. To that end they were to spend a weekend together once a month; keep an annual retreat; and attend a fortnight's summer school each year. The intention that younger graduates should spend time studying rooted in the industrial world (which Robinson had earlier advocated) did not come to pass in the context of the Southwark Ordination Scheme, but has subsequently become quite common.

In March 1960 the Central Advisory Council for the Ministry gave its approval to the Scheme. When Stockwood presented his plans to Diocesan Conference in June there was little to amend or add. He stressed the shortage of clergy, and the need to tap new sources. He proposed interchange of ordinands with theological colleges; in the event this proved impracticable. He again made plain his concern for the industrial areas.

> It is possible that if we can find suitable men who belong to these areas and understand their culture and outlook, they, if they are ordained, will find ways and means of communicating the Gospel to their fellows... The Southwark Scheme, in addition to preparing people for a full time professional ministry, is partly designed to cater for the training of such [worker] priests.[3]

He considered it necessary to impose a 5 year rule, that priests trained through the Scheme should be bound to serve their first five years in the diocese (unless the Bishop gave exceptional permission). The costs of the scheme would be small, and candidates might be expected to bear them from their earnings in secular employment.

When the course began in September 1960, thirty one men – out of 62 who had applied to be admitted to the Southwark Ordination Training Scheme – had been accepted by the Bishop. They were all from Southwark Diocese; men from other dioceses were not at this stage permitted to join the course. At the start they all met with Robinson at Dartmouth House. Six of the men had only attended primary schools, eighteen secondary schools and seven were graduates. Eight hoped to exercise a part time ministry and twelve to work full time. Ten would be prepared to do either. One was undecided. The great majority of the men were professional or managerial; there were in addition four clerks, an electrical engineer, a student and a London City Missioner. Though the course was intended for men of every churchmanship most evangelicals would not consider training in this way. That was later remedied. Robinson would have liked the course to be ecumenical from the start, and to train women as well as men, and lay people as well as those to be ordained, but he was persuaded to be content for the time being with what he, primarily, had pioneered – a theological college without walls. Lectures were held twice weekly in the Chapter House and, later, there was a service of Holy Communion every week in the Cathedral. The first Principal was Stanley Evans and the first Vice-Principal, from 1961, Frank Colquhoun. Benedicta Whistler was a very pastorally minded Bursar. Her work earned her the Lambeth degree of Master of Literature in 1978.

An influential conference on the ministry was held in June 1960 at Keble College, Oxford, which Robinson chaired. The record was entitled *New Ways with the Ministry* and Robinson contributed an essay *Taking the Lid off the Church's Ministry*. He drew attention to three barriers in the ministry. There was the professional line; this should be overcome by a greater range of non-stipendiary ministry. There was the clergy line; this should be overcome by abolition of the legal distinction between clergy and laity and by recognition of the distinctive functions within the Body. And there was the sex line. These were subjects that he was to develop more fully later.

In 1961 Robinson's *On Being the Church in the World* was published. In the address *The Priesthood of the Church* he pleaded for a renewed recognition of the whole church in priestly function. The whole church, the laity as well as the ordained, had a role in the liturgy. It was in the whole church in the priestly work of absolution that a man or woman might be delivered from the isolation of sin into the renewing fellowship of the Holy Spirit. It was the whole church, the healing *community*, not just the ordained, that ministered the priestly function of healing. In *The House Church and the Parish Church*, an address given to theological students, he strongly advocated house churches. His use of the New Testament was here, surprisingly, rather dubious, and his argument really only came to life when he spoke of what he had seen in Ernest Southcott's parish in Halton, Leeds. Robinson wrote that he believed the development of the church in the house to be the single most important thing that was happening in the Church of England at that time. But he also reiterated, prophetically enough, the need for a supplemental non-professional ministry.

Robinson contributed an essay *A New Model of Episcopacy* to Bishop Glyn Simon's symposium *Bishops*. In the light of biblical theology he asked for a focus on episcope, rather than episcopacy, the functional rather than the organisational; in the light of the ecumenical movement he asked that episcope be recognised as a function of the whole church, not just bishops; and in the light of the liturgical movement he asked that the bishop be recognised as having his true function in the liturgy together with the priests and deacons and the whole people of God. A bishop was to be the focus, not the exhaustive repository, of episcope. Robinson was opposed to the multiplication of provinces and dioceses, but he looked instead for episcopal team ministries, for e.g. London and Southwark. He would have approved of area bishops. He hoped for considerably more bishops, six, for example, in the Diocese of Southwark even as it was in the 1960's.

In an article *Fresh Thinking about Vocation to the Ordained Ministry* James wrote that every local church ought in some way to supply its own ministry.

Supposing every local church were asked each year to put forward the names of men and women who would be asked to consider ordination – ordination at first to the diaconate only – at first, and many ought not to be encouraged to think of the priesthood as their ultimate destination. The diaconate would be the order to which they were called for life. They would all at first be licensed to serve only at the local church or at the most in the local Rural Deanery... From the deacons from time to time men would be asked to be priests. The local church would be asked to nominate them, but their nominations would by no means always be accepted. No man would become either deacon or priest unless he had accepted considerable training for the ordained ministry. He would have to attend a C.A.C.T.M. selection board, which would have regard to the local ministry he was being asked to undertake. The bishop of the diocese would have as one of his chief responsibilities the guidance of congregations as to the type of men and women they should nominate. It would be quite natural for many of those ordained to their locality to ask to become full-time workers in the ordained ministry, especially at the age of retirement, but this would by no means be the objective for all. Indeed the full-time worker would be the exception. There would be a great need for diocesan training centres (such as that established at Bletchingley, Surrey, by the Diocese of Southwark,) but training of older men, men mostly married and with families, would, of course, take a different form from the somewhat monastic theological college training of the present clergy.[4]

This was a remarkable adumbration of the non-stipendiary ministry and especially of the local ordained ministry.

As Director of Lay Training Douglas Rhymes had a great concern for the ministry of the laity; he contributed to *Layman's Church*. Of the place of the laity in a parish and a layman's choice he wrote:

> He can either develop a kind of dual standard, one for his
> life in the Church and another for his week-day life in the
> world, keeping the two strictly apart and adapting the world's
> standard of values for his daily life and the Church's
> standards for his church life; or he can try to be aware of
> and to express the relevance of the Christian faith to the
> very problems, difficulties and standards of the world in
> which he lives and works: to voice and incarnate Christ's
> relevance to the whole range of human life ... If our faith is
> not relevant to our daily life in the world and in the parish,
> then it is no use; and if we cannot be Christians in our work,
> in the neighbourhood, in our political decisions, then we
> had better stop being Christians. A piety reserved for
> Sundays is no message for this age.[5]

A layman has to be able to stand in the faith over against the
values of the neighbourhood; the function of the layman is to be
prophetic about the world in which he lives; the world (even at
the parochial level) is the sphere in which the church is to be
involved in service, not the church structures themselves.

Rhymes, together with Cecilia Goodenough, pioneered the
development of lay ministry in the diocese; Rhymes made it his
business to learn from the laity what training they themselves
felt they needed (which he had a genius for eliciting). It proved
to be not simply training to be faithful members of the parish
church but training to meet responsibly as Christians the
complexities of the secular world. A later member of the training
team reckoned the parish weekends at Wychcroft and the lay
leadership courses in a class of their own. Not that every parish
or deanery was willing to accept such training, for polarisations
had already developed in the diocese; but for the many who did
it was very rewarding.

Of the thirty-one ordinands who began to study with the

Southwark Ordination Course in September 1960 thirteen were ready to be made deacons in Southwark Cathedral at the Michelmas ordination in 1963. Some had dropped out for reasons of health; some had transferrred to residential theological colleges; and some had decided that they did not have a vocation to the ordained ministry. Of those who completed the course five were to continue to earn their living in secular work and eight were to become full-time curates in the Diocese of Southwark. They agreed that the course had been testing. One student said, 'Without God's grace it simply could not be done. There are four examinations – three which last three hours each and one which takes six hours – that, on top of a full time job.' These academic demands had however a price – that the course became a non-starter for working class inner city men with blue collar jobs and families. The Southwark Ordination Course had reached its first fulfilment. In 1965 the Course received its full recognition by the Central Advisory Council for the Ministry and men from other dioceses, including Rochester, Guildford, London, Chelmsford and St. Alban's, began to be admitted. Representatives of other dioceses were invited to serve on the Council. The first woman, Una Kroll, a doctor and the mother of four children, was enrolled on the course in 1967 to train as a non-stipendiary deaconess-worker. The first student not an Anglican, a Methodist, was enrolled in 1974. Later United Reformed Church and Roman Catholic students were admitted. In 1968 Southwark Ordination Course men (together with Ken Ramsay) formed a special chapter of priest-workers. A priest baker, David Wilson, was elected dean.

In 1964 Stockwood appointed a Director of Pastoral Counselling for the diocese, the Revd. Maurice Clarke. The Canon Missioner, Gordon Davies, had begun seminars on Clinical Theology and Pastoral Counselling, introducing counselling skills and psychology, and young priests had been introduced to these topics as part of their post-ordination training.

Davies worked closely with Dr. Frank Lake. As the groups in the diocese developed (and Lake took a personal interest, often coming to South London and using Gilmore House as his base) Robinson perceived the need for their direction by a priest full time and Clarke was appointed. He had been trained in psychology at London University and had spent a year at the Pastoral Theology Centre at Nottingham. His brief was to travel round the diocese consulting with priests who were helping their parishioners with personal problems, offering a second opinion when asked for. It was hoped eventually to start a centre in the diocese. Close liason was to be established with the medical profession, social workers, hospital almoners and family planners. This development, the application of psychiatry in a religious context, had its consequences and inevitably led to reinterpretation of the sexual teachings of the church.

Leslie Paul, a sociologist with wide knowledge of the Church, published his report on *The Deployment and Payment of the Clergy* in 1964. It had had its inception in the Keble Conference, of which Robinson had been the chairman; that had led to a resolution of Church Assembly and in turn to Paul's commission. Among the report's recommendations were: that ordinands should accept direction for the first five years of their ministry; that the freehold should be transformed into a leasehold; that there should be major parishes with colleges of clergy together with group and team ministries; that freehold or leasehold should be extinguished at the age of 70; that there should be one common stipendiary system; and that patronage should be transformed into a staffing or appointments advisory system. Robinson received it with enthusiasm and spoke to it in Church Assembly a month after its publication – 'a masterly Report in itself' which 'represented a moment of truth for the Church of England'. But he did not regard it as radical enough. It did not go far enough in assimilating the pay and pensions of dignitaries to the rest of the clergy, nor in integrating the Church Commissioners with the responsible organs of the Church (he was prophetic there). He said that the Report was about the most radical reformation that there was a hope of getting through, and it was about the least radical required if the Church was to survive. Stockwood also supported the Report. Stacey, who was a key figure in the Keble Conference Group, was a keen advocate. He saw the need for overcoming haphazard decision making and for planning for the diocese as a whole.

> There is nothing more tiresome than when the bishop says one thing and his committees another... One of the most frustrating experiences in my life is sitting on a Diocesan Pastoral Reorganisation Committee. Again and again we are faced with making decisions involving the spending of thousands of pounds or the closing of a church without knowing what the overall plan and priorities for the area really are.[6]

A commission was set up following the Paul Report (the Morley Commission), which produced the report *Partners in Ministry* in 1967. James was a member of it. The Paul Report was only partially implemented – patronage reform only very partially; the freehold not at all; a compulsory retirement age was implemented; the institution of a Deployment and Payment Commission was not; and uniformity in remuneration to a very considerable degree. In the debate on the report in Church Assembly James spoke highly critically of the existing system of clergy deployment from his experience as Director of Parish and People meeting clergy throughout the country.

Church Assembly debated whether women might be priests in July 1967. By way of background, in February 1960 the then Archbishop of Canterbury, Geoffrey Fisher, had said that the ordination of women in the Church of England would be 'out of the question'. The motion was: 'That this Assembly, believing that there are no conclusive theological reasons why women should not be ordained to the priesthood but recognising that it would not be wise to take unilateral action at this time, welcomes further consideration of this matter by representatives of the Church of England and of the Methodist Church, in accordance with the request made by the Methodist Conference in July 1966.' When he spoke Robinson said he did not want to spend time arguing with those who thought there were conclusive theological objections to the ordination of women into the priesthood. Rather did he want to counter the arguments of those willing to have women priests, but not at that time. Ecumenically, an ordained ministry of women had been accepted by all those churches with which the Church of England hoped to enter into covenant. He quoted a Roman Catholic priest in France who believed women would be better priests than men and who hoped the Church of England would go forward. If it was against tradition for women to act as priests, Robinson continued, everywhere else in the modern world were they exercising a comparable responsibility. If it was argued that the majority of Church people had given little thought to the matter, he believed there had been a vast change in the atmosphere during the previous five years. If it was argued that it was false to suppose that the only way to exercise real ministry or vocation was by entering the professional priesthood, he would reply that unless the ends of responsibility were free and open all women's ministry for the Church would continue to be blighted.

Valerie Pitt, who had put in a plea for the ordination of women the previous year, proposed a following motion: 'That this Assembly, having weighed the arguments set down in the Report, judges that individual women who feel called to exercise the office and work of a priest in the Church shall now be considered, on the same basis as individual men, as candidates for Holy Orders.' She knew of no doctrine which did not recognise the call to the individual and the acceptance by the Church. A woman who felt such a call knew that not only would her call be rejected but that it would not even be considered. It was advanced that the order of creation revealed that women could not be priests. It was also advanced that a woman could not be head over men. She was head over five men, and her official title head of a division, so that she supposed she was in a state of sin by exercising that office. The Bishop of Chester had said 'We may feel that our Lord the Spirit is moving us in this direction.' There was such a thing as trying or testing the Spirit. Her motion merely asked that a woman who felt that she had a genuine vocation should have that vocation tested in the same way as a man. Both the substantive motion and the following motion were lost. A little later, in a letter of resignation from the Church Union, she protested, 'What I cannot respect is the unthinking conviction that many of your members have that, humanly speaking, any woman is inferior to any man and ought to be kept from sacred things.' Stockwood did not speak in this debate, although he had long advocated the ordination of women, from a time when he was one of few. He had addressed the Oxford University John Wesley Society on the subject shortly before the debate and said that while he welcomed the idea of women priests, he thought it was a 'lost cause' since too few women would come forward for ordination. 'To fight a long hard battle to get women admitted to the ministry, and then to find that only an infinitesimally small number of them want to be ordained, would be bad in these days when there are so many causes that one can fight for – causes that have a chance of being victorious.' He was in truth curiously equivocal about the matter, though when it came to it he was the first Church of England bishop to ordain a woman to the priesthood, Elizabeth Canham, in New York in 1981.

Robinson contributed a short article to *The Times* at the end of his time as Bishop of Woolwich under the title *Leadership as Letting Be.*

As I thought about it, I realized that almost any influence we [bishops] might have (we have little power) was not in pushing people around, but in letting be: allowing freedom to others to do their work, hindering hindrances, trying here a little there a little to remove the clogging restrictions and exhausting frustrations of law and money and plant – in other words, simply enabling people to be themselves, to grow and to fruit.

Now bishops and archdeacons and popes are not most notable for letting be. They are more associated with binding than with loosing. Despite the complete reversal of the world's idea of leadership of which Jesus spoke, the church, almost as much as the world, has learnt to live with the notion of leadership as something imposed from the top – authoritarian, paternalistic, however benevolent...

The world's idea of a leader is of a man who gets things done. Jesus' idea of a leader is of a man who is there above all to serve, to put himself out, to enable others to lead their community and to renew it, not from above or outside, but from within... For speaking of God himself the most fundamental category ... is that of "letting be". "And God said, Let there be ..." He is supremely the creator and sustainer of other beings freedom, the servant of his people. That is why he can most faithfully be revealed in the man for others who took a towel and girded himself.[7]

1. *Over the Bridge* June 1959 p 92
2. Eric James *A Life of Bishop John A.T. Robinson* 1987 p 92
3. Lambeth Palace Library Fisher Papers vol 256 ff 255f
4. *Prism* September 1962 pp 35f
5. Timothy Beaumont (ed) *Layman's Church* 1963 p 22
6. *Prism* June 1964 pp 8f
7. John A.T. Robinson *Christian Freedom in a Permissive Society* 1970 p 48

A New Morality

It was less than a year after John Robinson's consecration as Bishop of Woolwich that he was asked to appear as an expert witness in the trial of Penguin Books Ltd. for publishing an obscene article, *Lady Chatterley's Lover*. D.H. Lawrence's book had long been available in an expurgated form; Penguin Books were publishing it in full including a number of sexually explicit passages. Robinson found himself very willing to support the publication of the book in full, indeed convinced of the rightness of so doing. Stockwood did not debar him. Robinson very much wished to put forward a positive view of sex, which he saw in Lawrence; 'he was always straining to portray it as something sacred, in a real sense as an act of holy communion.' At the trial there was a considerable number of distinguished literary figures appearing for the defence. When Robinson was called he made his point:

> Clearly, Lawrence did not have a Christian valuation of sex [much had been made of Lady Chatterley's adulterous relationship with Mellors], and the kind of sexual relationship depicted in the book is not one that I would necessarily regard as ideal, but what I think is clear is that what Lawrence is trying to do is to portray the sex relationship as something essentially sacred.[1]

The jury found Penguin Books not guilty. Robinson instantly became a figure of huge publicity and controversy. The Archbishop of Canterbury, Geoffrey Fisher, censured him. From clergy in Southwark however there were only two letters opposed to his appearance in court and his evidence. One of them read:

> From the age of about nineteen years I have opposed to the best of my ability that which you defended in Court recently. If, presumably after invoking the name of a pure God, your

statements expressed your ideas of the truth, the whole truth, and nothing but the truth, upon the particular subject then under discussion, it seems but fair on my part to tell you that we are in opposite camps.[2]

No doubt Robinson explained the difficulty of expressing one's mind fully when giving evidence in court. The M.P. for Putney also protested vigorously.

Robinson found a doughty supporter in Valerie Pitt, who wrote a highly critical open letter to the Archbishop drawing on her own experience as a teacher of English Literature at Woolwich Polytechnic and sent it to *Time and Tide* for publication.

There can be little doubt that public opinion was ready for the change and that literary and artistic integrity called for the publication of *Lady Chatterley's Lover* without expurgations. Robinson was both perceptive and courageous in being ready to declare this publicly. The moral point, whether the publication of *Lady Chatterley's Lover* in full was obscene, i.e. liable to deprave and corrupt, now scarcely seems possible to answer save in the negative. When Robinson wrote that he believed that a serious injustice was being done to a great and creative work of literature, he was fully justified. Whether, though, he was altogether wise to stand as an expert witness when he had only begun to read Lawrence very shortly before is questionable; this, and an agenda of his own, setting forward a positive valuation of sexuality, may have led him to underestimate the paganism, sex as a religion, in Lawrence. It was no business of a Christian bishop to defend neo-paganism, even if inadvertently. Though it was certainly not Robinson's intention, the *Lady Chatterley's Lover* case was seen as a signal for permissiveness, moral permissiveness, a harbinger of the permissive society of the sixties.

As a parish priest Mervyn Stockwood had on occasion married divorced people in church since shortly after A.P.Herbert's Matrimonial Causes Bill in 1937, which permitted the clergy to do so. Soon after his arrival in Southwark Stockwood reminded the clergy of their legal right and also of the official attitude of the Church. It was a matter for their consciences; he did not wish to get involved. Although he did from time to time marry divorcees in his own chapel, he would not, in practice, give a bishop's licence for such a marriage. Some time later he asked in an anonymous questionnaire how many had married divorced people. Over a hundred replied positively. Early on in his episcopate he gave a divorced and remarried priest a living. Fisher protested.

World hunger was the subject of motions by Douglas Rhymes in Church Assembly in 1960 and again in 1963. His motions were passed unanimously. Technical assistance to developing countries was a subject that Stockwood spoke on in the House of Lords. He pointed to the need for an intermediate economics to be developed using quite simple industrial plant capable of village use. This is now pursued in many countries through the agency of the Intermediate Technology Development Group.

In letters and an article in the *Church Times*, Valerie Pitt raised the matter of the ethics of the Church Commissioners' investment policy. She pointed out that an investor owed responsibility both to the industry from which he derives his income and to the community whose welfare is bound up with that of industry and commerce. It was not obligatory to accept bids which, though financially attractive to the investor, might be harmful to industry. The Commissioners did not seem to recognise more than the security and respectability of the investment and its financial returns. In a further letter she wrote that though the Commissioners held in trust property of such a size and kind that its management had a perceptible social effect (she had earlier written of them as 'a City Power'), the Commissioners were, apparently, insensitive to the social responsibilities which devolved on them. She instanced their altogether inadequate provision of housing for the homeless (a concern also shared by

Nicolas Stacey). In a later article she drew attention to the ethical problems of investing in paternalistic concerns, where the Unions were resisted, or in firms which exercised a colour bar, or in banks which invested in South Africa. 'If we are to solve the ethical problems of our dependence on modern commerce (for this is what the Commissioners' financial policy involves), we have to find some way of living from our own resources.'

The Lower House of Convocation debated capital punishment in the October sessions of 1961. Rhymes spoke against its retention. He argued that it was unnecessary as a deterrent; that life imprisonment formed a satisfactory alternative punishment; and that it was unchristian to retain it for revenge. Robinson also spoke. In a moving speech he first referred to the lead given by the American Church and then went on to mention the story of Cain. 'They still talked of "the mark of Cain" branding a man as a murderer, but they did not remember it had been a saving mark to protect him from the retribution of society. What society did today in taking life was precisely what the Almighty had felt unable to bear in the case of Cain.' He continued, 'The death sentence said in effect, "There is nothing more we can do with this man; for his own sake or for society's sake we must put an end to his life. He is strictly unredeemable; we can only put him away." The Christian faith said "There is no man who is unredeemable; in Christ all men can be raised above the level of mere human nature and given the capacity to become the sons of God."'[3]

Stockwood proposed a motion calling for the abolition of capital punishment in the Upper House of Convocation in January 1962. He argued that a majority of countries had by then abolished it; that, quoting the Royal Commission of 1949, there was 'no clear evidence of any influence of the death penalty on the homicide rates'; that murderers could be imprisoned and even reclaimed instead of executed; that, even if abolition went beyond public opinion, the House of Commons, the elected representatives of the people of Britain, had already voted for it; and that, if it were said that abolition implied greater consideration for the offender than for the person against whom the offence had been committed, that was questionable. Murder was terrible and tragic but execution was no adequate compensation. The murderer should be reclaimed (he later gave testimony to that possibility from personal experience). The Christian concern was for repentance, forgiveness and reclamation. Christianity called for such sort of repudiation as did not hinder but rather facilitated its supreme interest in making a moral restoration. But that was the one thing which the death sentence made impossible; the death sentence was a denial of the Gospel, because it said of a man that in this life he was unredeemable and must be destroyed, and in doing so the State took to itself the prerogatives of God.' The bishops voted almost unanimously for the motion. In November 1965 capital punishment was abolished for an experimental period of five years. The abolition was made permanent in 1969.

Stockwood proposed a motion on the care of old people at the May 1962 sessions of Convocation. He pointed to the multiplicity of departments with which an old person might have to deal – the Housing Manager, the Medical Officer of Health, the Welfare Department, the National Assistance Board – and an old person might well be passed from one department to another. He quoted a Ministry of Health report, 'What is needed is one focal point in every place to which they can turn should assistance be needed or advice required.' That was eventually supplied after the Seebohm Report of 1968 in the Local Government and Social Services Act of 1970, whereby social services were centralised at local government level.

In the October 1962 sessions of Convocation Stockwood spoke in the Upper House against racial hatred and racial discrimination. Oswald Clark had spoken on the same subject in Church Assembly two years before, opposing all forms of racial bitterness and hatred and calling for Christian reconciliation. After the 1964 General Election Stockwood spoke out against the electors of Smethwick, where there had been a racist campaign. In a letter to *The Times* he quoted a statement from the World Council of Churches:

> We repeat with all the conviction at our command that any form of segregation based on race, colour or ethnic origin is contrary to the Gospel and is incompatible with the Christian doctrine of Man and with the nature of the Church of Christ. Whenever and wherever any of us Christians deny this by action or inaction we betray Christ and the fellowship which bears his name.[4]

Speaking in the House of Lords on Southern Rhodesia in 1968, Stockwood told of his vision of multi-racial unity. 'Yesterday morning, in a part of my diocese where there is a very large coloured minority, I was celebrating the Holy Communion and it was my joy and privilege to give the Sacrament to dozens of white and coloured people who knelt side by side at the Table. Then the mothers brought up their children again, both white and coloured, for me to bless them, and afterwards I had my refreshment with them. That is the vision which motivates me.' John Hay, a Canon of Jamaica Cathedral, had been appointed to work among West Indian immigrants. A special church would have been made available if it had been thought necessary, not to segregate, but to provide a church where West Indians would feel at home. For whatever reason this did not come to pass. The reception of black people in the churches varied from outright rejection to welcome; it was sometimes necessary for them to be persistent to find an accepted place in a congregation. They generally lacked confidence and authority and white people, even of goodwill, were therefore paternalistic. Housing was regularly a problem; on the whole black people had to seek their own solutions. Employment was easy in the earlier days, but became more difficult later. The schooling of the children of immigrants aroused concern. The Deputy Director of the Diocesan Board of Education, J.H.H. Coombes, writing in *The Bridge,* drew attention to difficulties of language, both for the children themselves and for communication with parents; difficulties of differing ways of exercising discipline; and difficulties arising from differences of religion. In particular he drew attention to the problem of discrimination in some areas if church schools insisted on excluding non-Christians. He concluded,

> I don't think we want to produce an integrated, multi-racial society with all immigrants assimilated into our own culture. We want them to develop their own culture – mellowed no doubt by contact with us – to be themselves.[5]

In general it must be said that even where there was goodwill among the white members of the churches there was little practical action.

Robinson had a chapter on morality in *Honest to God*, under the title *The New Morality*. He took the title from a document issued by the Supreme Sacred Congregation of the Holy Office in 1956, and though its use by that body was polemical, he was willing to accept it. Robinson made the contrast between supranaturalism and naturalism in ethics, as in doctrine. Supranaturalism looks to given rules in the church or the Bible with divine authentication, but is rigid and distorting; naturalism dispenses with God, but leads to relativism and subjectivism. What is needed is the one imperative, love alone, to meet each concrete situation. Therefore 'nothing can of itself always be labelled as "wrong".' This was expounded in relation to marriage and divorce and sexual intercourse before marriage, which conveyed a broadly libertarian sense in spite of Robinson's clear understanding that a deep love would preclude intercourse before marriage. He did not turn his back on guiding rules, the cumulative experience of Christian obedience. But he insisted on the priority of loving respect for persons, each unique individual person – unconditionally. 'Persons are more important even than standards.' Strangely, in all the initial furore over *Honest to God*, this chapter did not provoke much controversy.

Not long after the publication of *Honest to God* Rhymes preached a series of sermons at the Cathedral on the subject of sexual and marital morality. They were published in 1964 as *No New Morality*. He acknowledged his debt to Robinson and, though he put forward a somewhat more conservative viewpoint, there is no doubt which side he was on. Against the traditional pattern of moral law on the one hand and against the protest which insists that goodness is the fulfilment of a particular end, as, for instance, in Marxism, on the other, he held that there was a third view, 'which is that goodness is determined by the adequacy with which an individual is to live his life in its wholeness, so that the goodness of an action is determined by its place in the life of a person; that what is good and right is what provides for the deepest welfare of a particular person in a particular situation.' He drew on psychological insights and provided carefully worked out examples. He was well aware of the influence of secularity and stressed the inappropriateness of insisting on Christian morality for a secular society. Like Robinson, Rhymes propounded not a rule, but a relationship morality. He took his ideas further in an article in *New Christian* in 1966. He drew a distinction between the traditionalist view, concerned with what *ought* to be, and the majority of moral decisions, taking place in the realm of what *is*. In his view, in any given situation the *ideal* and the actual have to be the same, for the only *ideal* that is practicable is what is the most responsible thing to do in the given situation. What is positively bad is to hold up an ideal which cannot be actualised as a basis of conduct, for this is not to deal with the given at all but with a make-believe situation which does not exist. He illustrated his thesis by reference to the failed marriage and the position of the homosexual. The official position of the Church does nothing to help the people involved in either situation because it treats not with the situation as such but instead with an "Ideal" which is not within the given situation. When two people come for advice when their marriage has utterly and irretrievably broken down the question they are facing is not "How do I maintain the outward facade of what has ceased to be?" nor "How do I live a celibate life without future marriage?" These are not the ideals which bear any relevance whatsoever to their present condition. In preaching to them, both the tragedy of their broken marriage and the necessity now of never marrying again, or having any sexual relationship, the Church is not holding up an ideal. It is dealing in realm of make-believe which has no relation to the facts of the case. Rhymes turned also to homosexuality. The important moral question, and therefore the real and the ideal for the persons involved, is the *quality* of the relationship. To limit concern to whether or not there is a physical relationship is to deal in the realm of make-believe, for this is not really the question which concerns the homosexual. Anyone who has had dealings with homosexuals know that when two adult homosexuals come seeking advice they are not asking the question "How do I lead a complete celibate life?" but "How do I make of this a satisfactory relationship?" The Church does not deal with their real problem. It only treats them as if they were seeking voluntary celibacy, so creating a make-believe answer to a make-believe question. The article concluded by seeking to apply the same principles to business ethics and to international affairs.[6]

Robinson came back to 'the new morality' in a series of three lectures given in Liverpool Cathedral in October 1963, published as *Christian Morals Today*. They were something of an eirenicon – from conviction, not from expediency; he was careful to draw on the insights of both 'old' and 'new' in moral matters, which, he said, were complementary. He drew attention to the phenomenon of change in ethical judgements, e.g. those concerning war and peace, capital punishment, and suicide. If there are elements of fixity, there must also be elements of freedom, relativity, for ethics to respond to the ethos of their day. When he passed to the teaching of Jesus he insisted that it was not an ethical code, but rather pictures of the uncompromising demand which the Kingdom must make upon anyone who would respond to it. "The Sermon on the Mount does not say in advance, 'This is what in every circumstance or in any circumstance you must do', but 'This is the kind of thing which at any moment, if you are open to the absolute unconditional will of God, the Kingdom, or love, can demand of you'." Robinson sought to rebut the charge that 'the new morality' was individualistic, but the rebuttal was not very convincing. In his last lecture he said that the only true authority in ethics was an empirical one, starting from the data of actual personal relationships as they were. By well chosen examples (capital punishment and homosexuality) he showed how unsatisfactory it was to use isolated Biblical texts as authoritative answers to ethical situations. It was perhaps unfortunate that he should have returned to sex before marriage and divorce, which reinforced the impression that 'the new morality' was only concerned with personal relationships, when he wanted to show that it had a much wider ethical significance. He concluded with a plea for the priority of persons over principles. In *Christian Freedom in a Permissive Society* the lectures which formed *Christian Morals Today* were reprinted and an appendix added. He returned to sexuality once more, a repetition which again seems unfortunate. His optimism over sexual matters is shown by this paragraph:

Sooner or later we are likely to reach the situation when parenthood will be completely voluntary. Indeed, instead of taking *ad hoc* steps to prevent conception, we may reach the opposite position, where immunity is the norm, except when and as men and women deliberately choose to have children. Moreover, I find it difficult to believe that we cannot remove the scourge of V.D. as we have already, virtually, removed the scourge of T.B. Indeed, if it was a killer, I suspect we should already be on the way to doing so. Furthermore, with the fears of conception and infection lifted, the stigma of detection, which induces furtiveness, insecurity and guilt, and condemns the possibility of deep, free, and therefore truly loving, relationships outside a certain area of society's approval, is likely to disappear rapidly.[7]

The House of Lords debated Homosexual Offences in May 1965. Stockwood made a moving speech in favour of reform of the law, instancing two sad cases from his personal knowledge of men driven to suicide under the threat of police prosecution for homosexual offences. Prison, he said, was the worst possible treatment for the homosexual. It was surely as absurd as locking up an alcoholic in the bar of a public house. When the Sexual Offences Bill came before the Lords later the same month, Stockwood again declared himself in favour of reform. 'The fundamental point at issue here is not whether we can or cannot stomach the thought of this or that type of sexual behaviour; it is whether or not we believe that true morality, and the best way of cultivating personal responsibility, is to be found through freedom or through compulsion, and whether or not we believe that the present law on this subject does more harm than good.' Robinson too held that the criminality of homosexual acts should be abolished. He had joined the executive committee of the Homosexual Law Reform Society in 1960.

In 1966 Robinson was persuaded to turn his mind to the matter of abortion law reform in a lecture delivered to the Abortion Law Reform Association. In faithfulness to the method of *The New Morality* he began, not with rule, but by seeking what in the situation was most loving, most agapeistic. He made the point that compelled decisions were not moral decisions. 'The place of the law is 'to protect the freedom to decide, which must lie ultimately, if it is to be a moral decision, with the woman herself.'His plea was to maximise knowledge, especially on the medical matters involved; to maximise freedom, to enable genuine moral decisions to be made; and to abolish criminality. In spite of his evident personal abhorrence of abortion, his argument was understood to be in favour of permissiveness. He did lay himself open to this by restricting the protective function of the law to freedom of choice and failing to declare its wider functions of protection.

Christian Freedom in a Permissive Society also contained an essay on obscenity. Robinson noted that there were different possible strands to obscenity – eroticism, the obscenity of violence as well as the obscenity of sex, and pornography. He wished to give full freedom to eroticism, indeed to commend it. Obscenity, he observed, was impossible to define. What one person found depraving and corrupting, another did not. What was publicly offensive might reasonably be restrained. Nevertheless the basic presupposition was freedom. Pornography might be unhealthy, but he did not think it was the function of the law to prohibit it as such. Freedom was the most precious commodity. The law was to protect it rather than to prohibit it.Robinson's arguments concerning abortion law reform and obscenity, with their emphasis on freedom and personal responsibility, were very similar to the argument used by Stockwood in favour of homosexual law reform.

1. Eric James *A Life of Bishop John A.T. Robinson* 1987 pp 92, 95
2. Ibid p 102
3. Chronicle of Convocation Lower House 5th October 1961 p 634
4. *The Times* 27th October 1964
5. *The Bridge* March 1969
6. *New Christian* 5th May 1966
7. John A.T. Robinson *Christian Freedom in a Permissive Society* 1970 p 48

Outcomes

For *Honest to God* and its effect on many who read it Robinson himself seized on the word 'release'. Although there were many who were distressed by the book, there were also perhaps as many who found intellectual and spiritual release through it and there certainly were those who were brought back to the worshipping life of the Church through reading it. More widely it loosened up theological thinking and paved the way to a much greater intellectual freedom in the church which was overdue; it provided an opening to feminist theology, black theology and liberation theology, all of which have been of importance.

Two themes from *Honest to God* are of contemporary significance. Robinson had a deep concern that theology should respect persons. So he could write, 'compassion for *persons* overrides all law', and again, 'love is the end of the law precisely because it *does* respect persons.' Concern for persons needs to be balanced by rules, but a religion dominated by rules loses sight of that for which the rules exist, concern for the flesh and blood neighbour.

Even more characteristic of South Bank Religion was the concern for the secular. Again Robinson wrote 'The test of worship is how far it makes us *more sensitive* to the 'beyond in the midst', to the Christ in the hungry, the naked, the homeless and the prisoner. Only if we are *more likely* to recognise him there after attending an act of worship is that worship Christian rather than a piece of religiosity in Christian dress' [1]. Robinson himself never lost his concern for the secular world, and it was typical of the movement to be firmly in touch with it, offering it service and hearing what it was saying in order to take from it what was good into the life of the church. This has relevance now given theologies which are antagonistic to the secular. There is a standing temptation for the church to shrink within the boundaries of its own life to find security. The Church is faithful to the gospel only if there is also openness to the world outside.

Robinson was a convinced advocate of the Liturgical Movement. He commended the parish communion, which, though adopted by some parishes in England some years before, was still not common. By the end of his time as Bishop of Woolwich many more parishes had accepted it. He also liked to celebrate in the westward position, which generally went with the parish communion. Both he and Stockwood looked for churches planned in accordance with the Liturgical Movement, churches with a free standing altar surrounded by worshippers whom the celebrant faced. Several churches were built on this principle. Though Southwark did not initiate these changes, it certainly forwarded them. By now considerable numbers of churches have been and still are being built or re-ordered on this central plan with the community gathered round the altar.

A further fruit of the liturgical movement was the production of music which the whole congregation could sing rather than just a choir; this was the explicit purpose of a notable church composer, Patrick Appleford in Camberwell. Congregational music has now become necessary, as fewer parishes have a formal choir. Robinson also argued that children should be admitted to communion before confirmation by virtue of their baptism. This practice has also been adopted by a good number of churches.

As well as change in the setting of the liturgy there was change in its language. Stockwood commended modern translations of the Bible; Robinson was himself a translator for the *New English Bible*. The use of modern translations of the Bible has now long been authorised and is common. There was also change in the form of the liturgy. Stockwood set up his own diocesan liturgical committee, which produced services for Holy Week – economical, but to the point, following the traditional usages of the week. The committee also produced a eucharistic liturgy, which made the structure of the eucharist clear and which, by contrast with the Book of Common Prayer, rehearsed all the acts of God, not just the death of Christ. The most striking liturgical changes came from Eric James and Nicolas Stacey in the baptismal liturgies which they prepared. They were written with great simplicity and directness.

The first tentative steps to liturgical reform were embodied in Series II in 1967. That led on to a modern language liturgy, Series III, in 1971 and in due course to the Alternative Service Book of 1980, which lasted 20 years. That has now been replaced by Common Worship. This last is a work of considerable complexity with a host of options. The liturgical principles of simplicity and directness of the 1960's, which were also the principles of the Book of Common Prayer in its day, have been rejected by its compilers. Common Worship Daily Prayer seems more suited to the needs of religious communities than to those of the Church as a whole.

The bringing into being of the Southwark Ordination Course, training ordinands non-residentially, has generally been reckoned a major achievement of the Diocese of Southwark in the 1960's. A highly innovatory scheme was given full recognition by the Central Advisory Council for the Church's Ministry after only five years of operation. Forty years after its inception there were as many as twelve similar non-residential courses, covering virtually all the country. More ordinands are now training through non-residential institutions than through residential colleges. A significant proportion of the former are ordained to a non-stipendiary ministry. This has meant that those starting their ministries have often been older than was previously the case and that priests working in secular employment have brought that experience to their ministerial work. Stockwood hoped that men from the shop floor would train for the priesthood through the Southwark Ordination Course, but the academic requirements, on which he insisted from the first, as well perhaps as other social factors, have effectively debarred them. Stockwood and Robinson hoped that in many instances the centre of the ministries of priests in secular employment would be in their places of work, but they underestimated the difficulties of this.

There have been criticisms of the academic standards of non-residential courses. The Southwark Ordination Course has had students ranging in academic background from primary school education only to a doctorate in divinity. As has just been noted Robinson and Stockwood required high standards; nevertheless with few members of staff and limited time for tuition this is hard of achievement. There can be no going back on non-residentiary training. It will be most effective where there is prioritisation, so that what is fundamental is covered thoroughly even at the cost of comprehensive coverage of all that might be desired.

Eric James put forward the idea of a local ordained ministry. An experimental scheme was tried at Bethnal Green in the Diocese of London in 1972 and a further experimental scheme in Newington in the Diocese of Southwark in 1981. A more permanent scheme for the training and work of local ordained ministers was begun in 1992 in Southwark. James saw it as the business of the local church to put forward names for this ministry; here lies its strength, for it is known members of the congregation who are recommended for ordination in the light of their ability to declare the faith and to offer pastoral care to other members of the congregation. There is a growing number of ordained local ministers, and their presence is changing the shape of the ministry overall.

A much greater change, with, for the Church of England, astonishing swiftness, has been the ordination of women. Perhaps the swiftness represented a widespread feeling within the country as a whole of the appropriateness of the change It seems unlikely that, when Robinson and Valerie Pitt advocated the ordination of women to the priesthood in a Church Assembly debate in July 1967, taking up the work of such bodies as the Anglican Group for the Ordination of Women to the Historic Ministry of the Church, many in that meeting anticipated that it would be a reality in less than thirty years. But it has become so. Among the stipendiary priests there are now 1140 women compared with 8398 men; women priests are thus a substantial minority and obviously here to stay. The cost has been some alienation within the church, and a weakening of the Catholic wing. But if priests working in secular employment have changed and enriched the pattern of ministry, women priests have much more so.

Robinson, and Douglas Rhymes too, looked for a personal, relational, rather than a rule morality. Robinson was not opposed to traditional moral guidance, but wished, in moral thinking, to prioritise the effects on the person concerned. In Convocation he spoke movingly about suicide, pointing to the responsibility of society for such situations, often as great or even greater than that of the individuals who took their own lives. He also spoke movingly (as also did Stockwood) on the subject of capital punishment, which, he said, denied the possibility of a person's redemption. The insight that the personal is always to be considered in moral decisions and that a rule morality by itself is inadequate is of lasting value.

Valerie Pitt raised the question of the morality of the Church Commissioners' investment policy. This was taken up in the 1980's in connection with investments in South Africa, leading to a court case in 1990 in which Bishop Richard Harries, of Oxford, asked for a declaration that the Church Commisioners were obliged too have regard to the object of promoting the Christian faith through the established Church of England and that they might not act in a manner which would be incompatible with that object. The court rejected the declaration on the grounds that it was too general. However the court did not criticise the controversial policy of refraining from investment in South Africa, leaving the door open to take up similar situations of limited generality in the future.

Stockwood, in the context of homosexual law reform (homosexuality in the church and homosexual priests – of which there were some – were then not an issue) argued that true morality and personal responsibility demanded freedom, not the compulsion of the law. Robinson used much the same argument in connection with abortion law reform and the law of obscenity. The place of the law is to protect the freedom to decide. Given the protecting power of the law, then the shift of responsibility to the individual is good, and in a multicultural society, of which there is now much greater awareness, it is increasingly necessary. Robinson gave it as his conviction that, 'It is precisely a sign of a civilised society that it progressively substitues the free processes of social judgement for the sanctions of penal repression'.

'South Bank Religion' has been held responsible for the permissive society of the 1960's. The permissive society was in fact a social phenomenon reflecting the greater prosperity and greater independence among young people at that time, and their increasing secularization. The Beatles did not owe anything to Southwark. Robinson was not permissive; he abhorred abortion, for instance, and did not welcome sex before marriage. Charged with permissivness he replied by entitling a book *Christian Freedom in a Permissive Society.* That is what he believed in.

As Mervyn Stockwood came to Southwark as Bishop in May 1959, he plainly had a missionary purpose; in his enthronement sermon, a very outward looking one, he called for deeply commited Christians who would be outgoing in the secular world. That missionary purpose John Robinson shared; 'I want God to be real in the modern world.' Their episcopate saw a host of new ideas and innovations with that aim ; inevitably some were misleading or failures, but many were not and were and are of benefit not merely to the Diocese of Southwark but to the Church of England as a whole. 'South Bank Religion' was born in controversy and still is controversial. It came as something of a surprise to the author to hear a bishop conservative by disposition say that he thought it 'of God'.

1. John A. T.Robinson *Honest to God* 1963 p. 90

Bibliography

Appleford, Patrick, *Mass of the Five Melodies*. Josef Weinberger, 1961.

Archbishop's Commission on the Organisation of the Church by Dioceses in London and the South East of England, *Diocesan Boundaries*. Church Information Office, 1967.

Archbishops' Commission on Intercommunion, *Intercommunion Today*. Church Information Office, 1968.

Beaumont, Geoffrey, *20th Century Folk Mass*. Josef Weinberger, 1956.

Beaumont, Timothy (ed), *Layman's Church*. Lutterworth Press, 1963.

Carr-Gomm, Richard, *Push on the Door, An Autobiography*. Carr-Gomm Society, 1979.

Colquhoun, Frank, *Parish Prayers*. Hodder and Stoughton, 1967.

Commission appointed by the Archbishops of Canterbury and York, *Sharing of Churches*. CIO, 1966.

Commission on the Deployment and Payment of the Clergy, *Partners in Ministry*. Church Information Office, 1967.

Cooke, Jenny, *Upon this rock*. Hodder and Stoughton, 1989.

Cope, Gilbert (ed), *Making the Building Serve the Liturgy Studies in the Re-ordering of Churches*. A.R. Mowbray, 1962.

De-la-Noy, Michael, *Mervyn Stockwood A Lonely Life*. Mowbrays, 1996.

Earle, Nick, *What's Wrong with the Church?* Penguin Books,1961.

Evans, Stanley G., *The Nuclear Deterrent and the Christian Conscience*. 1962.

Evans, Stanley G., *The Church in the Back Streets*. A.R. Mowbray, 1962.

Evans, Stanley G., *In Evening Dress to Calvary*. SCM Press, 1965.

Evans, Stanley G.,*The Social Hope of the Christian Church*. Hodder and Stoughton,1965.

Group appointed by the Archbishop of Canterbury, *Putting Asunder A divorce law for contemporary society*. SPCK, 1966.

Hammond, Peter, *Liturgy and Architecture*. Barrie and Rockliff, 1960.

Institute for the Study of Worship and Religious Architecture of the University of Birmingham, *Cathedral and mission*. 1969.

James, Eric, *Odd Man Out?* Hodder and Stoughton,1962.

James Eric, *The Roots of the Liturgy.* Prism Pamphlet, 1962.

James, Eric, *A Life of Bishop John A.T. Robinson Scholar, Pastor, Prophet.* Collins, 1987.

James, Eric (ed), *Spirituality for Today.* SCM Press, 1968.

Jones, C.P.M. (ed), *A manual for Holy Week.* SPCK, 1967.

Morris, John Richard, *New Ways with the Ministry.* Faith Press, 1960.

Paul, Leslie, *The Deployment and Pay of the Clergy.* Church Information Office, 1964.

Peters, John, *Frank Lake, the man and his work.* Darton Longman and Todd, 1989.

Rhymes, Douglas A., *No New Morality.* Constable, 1964.

Rhymes, Douglas A., *Prayer in the Secular City.* Lutterworth Press, 1967.

Robinson, John A.T., *Liturgy Coming to Life.* A.R. Mowbray, 1960.

Robinson, John A.T., *On Being the Church in the World.* SCM Press, 1960.

Robinson, John A.T., *Honest to God.* SCM. Press, 1963.

Robinson, John A.T., *Christian Morals Today.* SCM. Press, 1964.

Robinson, John A.T., *The New Reformation?* SCM. Press, 1965.

Robinson, John A.T., *But That I Can't Believe.* Collins, 1967.

Robinson, John A.T., *Exploration into God.* SCM Press, 1967.

Robinson, John A.T., *Christian Freedom in a Permissive Society.* SCM Press, 1970

Robinson, John A.T. and Edwards, David L., *The Honest to God Debate.* SCM. Press,1963.

Robinson, Ruth, *Seventeen Come Sunday.* SCM Press, 1966.

Simon, Glyn (ed), *Bishops.* Faith press, 1961.

Southcott, E.W. *The Parish Comes Alive.* A.R.Mowbray, 1956.

Stacey, Nicolas, *Who Cares.* Blond, 1971.

Stockwood, Mervyn, *Cambridge Sermons.* Hodder and Stoughton, 1961.

Stockwood, Mervyn, *Bishop's Journal.* A.R. Mowbray, 1964.

Stockwood, Mervyn, *Chantonbury Ring.* Hodder and Stoughton Sheldon Press,1982.

Swann, Donald, *Requiem for the Living.* J. Curwen and Sons, 1972.

Torry, Malcolm A.N., *Over the Bridge A History of the South London Industrial Mission*. Unpublished thesis.

Wadderton Group, *Alive in God's World.* Church Information Office, 1968.

Index